C000174555

BANKING 2020:
A VISION FOR THE FUTURE

BANKING 2020:
A VISION FOR THE FUTURE

Edited by Steve Tolley

Contributors: Steve Baker MP, Sharon Bowles MEP (with Damian Horton), Vicky Ford MEP, Mark Garnier MP, David Jackman, Syed Kamall MEP, Baroness Kramer, Andrea Leadsom MP, Chris Leslie MP, Andy Love MP, John Mann MP & John Thurso MP.

Introduction by: Steve Tolley and Tony Greenham

First edition published in paperback in Great Britain in 2013 by
nef (the new economics foundation)
3 Jonathan Street
London
SE11 5NH
www.neweconomics.org
E-mail: info@neweconomics.org
Telephone: +44 (0)20 7822 6300

British Library Cataloguing in Publication Data: a catalogue record for this book is available from the British Library.

ISBN: 978 1 90850 636 8

registered charity number 1055254

The new economics foundation supports The Forest Stewardship Council [FSC], the leading international forest certification organization. All **nef** book titles are printed on FSC certified paper.

Cover design and art direction danfarleydesign.co.uk
Typeset by Hewer Text UK Ltd, Edinburgh, Scotland EH10 7DU
Production management Eddepro, West Sussex RH12 3DQ
Copy edited by Mary Murphy

Printed and bound in Great Britain by TJ International, Padstow PL28 8RW

ACKNOWLEDGEMENTS

Firstly, the editor would like to thank Rosie Clarke who gave valuable advice and put up with frequent ramblings and constant questions during this book's gestation period.

Secondly, thanks to the contributors and their researchers and assistants who made this book possible: Bridget Beechey, Jessica Cole, Harry Cooper, Jane Dickens, Peter Edwards, Agnieszka Kandouci, Marc Pooler, Parisa Smith, Amelia Viney, James Walsh, Alex Wentworth and others.

I'd also like to thank everyone at **nef** involved in putting the book and its launch event together: Tony Greenham, Carys Afoko, Jessie Barnard, Cam Ly and Ross Haig. Thanks also go to Mary Murphy, Angie Greenham, Gavin and Andrew at Hewer Text and Dan Farley at Dan Farley Design for invaluable assistance with editing, proofing, design, layout and production control for Banking 2020: A vision for the future.

Lastly, thanks to Sarah McDowell, without whom none of this would have happened.

Steve Tolley, Editor, June 2013

CONTENTS

2020 BANKING: A VISION FOR THE FUTURE

by Steve Tolley and Tony Greenham

Put yourself in the shoes of a bank's chief executive. Consider what your industry has been through since 2007: the panic of the initial crisis; the embarrassment of bailouts to prevent collapse; being the target of the public's anger at having to foot the bill; and (presumably) the guilt over the part played by banks in Europe's continuing economic crisis – both in terms of the public costs of keeping banks going and the impact of predatory speculation on struggling economies.

After going through all that, as chief executive, you would expect changes. Under current plans, by 2019 banks will have ring-fenced their retail arms and will be operating under new prudential requirements. A slew of rules, mostly from Europe, but also from the now defunct Financial Services Authority will have changed the way banks do business. And, of course, this new banking landscape will be watched over by the new UK regulators and the European supervisory authorities (ESAs).

But is all this change in the right direction, and is it enough? Whatever the outcome of current proposals, they are not – according to this book's contributors – the end of the matter. In the essays that follow, we are presented with 12 politicians and regulators' contrasting visions of what banking should look like in 2020. As the boss, you might take from the collection the lesson that the appetite for deeper-reaching change amongst citizens and their representatives continues to grow; reform ain't over yet.

Consensus and beyond

Taking our 12 contributors' pieces together, can we discern the outlines of a unified vision of banking in 2020? Some parts of the landscape are sharply in focus while others are hazy.

Competition, diversity, and customer choice
What seems most clear is the idea of the customer taking centre stage. It might seem remarkable that any consumer industry would need to be exhorted to put its customers first, but this is the starting point for many of our contributors.

There are various elements to this. There is, for example, a chorus of approval for introducing far more competition and diversity into the retail banking market. Susan Kramer, John Thurso, Mark Garnier, and Chris Leslie want customers to have a much broader choice between different kinds of banking institutions. The alternatives they point to include specialist lenders with deep knowledge of their markets, community banks and mutuals, local banks that are much closer to the communities they serve, and new business models such as peer-to-peer (P2P) lending. However, many authors point out that not enough has been done so far to boost competition, arguing that for choice to be effective, customers must be able to exercise it easily and conveniently. Andrea Leadsom argues forcefully that only full bank account number portability will do the job. Today's mobile phone users would find the idea of not being able to move their phone number to a different provider quite bizarre. Tomorrow's bank account holders will feel the same.

Andy Love and others highlight the need for inclusivity. Every citizen, he says, must be well served with low cost transactional banking services in order to fully participate in the modern, digital economy. Large banks have a key role in delivering Basic Bank Accounts (BBAs) and also in supporting and partnering with local community banks to reach under-served communities. Kramer, Leslie, and Love consider greater disclosure and transparency about where banks offer their services, and to whom, necessary to achieve this goal. To this John Mann adds the need for greater transparency about the industry's use of tax havens.

Another essential element of competition is the free entry and, equally importantly, free exit of banking firms from the market. Our contributors see progress in this area, but want more. An end to taxpayers being forced to bail out systemically vital banks is key. Sayed Kamall and John Mann see a complete split between retail and investment banking as important. Steve Baker argues that state backing for banks results inevitably from our system of state-backed fiat money, and proposes a model of competing currencies whose desirability rests on the credibility of the banks that issue them.

Shifting incentives and fixing the culture

Culture and ethics are considered by a number of contributors. David Jackman calls for values-led practice both in banks and regulators. Recognising the interaction of ownership, incentives, and values, he calls for a restriction of voting rights to solely long-term shareholders and a greater voice for other stakeholders in the governance of banking institutions. This should address short-termism and empower managers to balance the needs of customers, employees, shareholders, and citizens. Leslie proposes a more comprehensive system of licencing for bankers, enabling them to be held to account for their integrity and competence in the same way as other professions.

The misalignment of incentives for managers underlies calls for more restrained levels of remuneration that better track performance. Baker, Kamall, and Thurso conclude that a return to unlimited liability for directors, or the return of certain activities to unlimited liability partnerships, would be the most reliable way to realign the interests of owners, customers, and managers.

Some authors address the ever more lengthy, expensive, and complex channels between investors and borrowers. For Sharon Bowles and Damian Horton, exposing purveyors of complexity to the full legal liabilities of their losses would curb this tendency, but a more fundamental improvement in investment would result from taking advantage of innovations in crowd funding. The more direct involvement of retail investors brings knowledge, accountability, and transparency into investment allocation. Bowles and Horton also advocate that businesses in general develop a more decentralised corporate structure that allows people to invest directly in local subsidiaries of large companies.

Reshaping regulation
If our policymakers are strident about the need to reform banking institutions and banking culture, they are no less critical of the performance of regulators. Jackman points out the perverse consequences of Basel capital adequacy rules, while Kamall laments the loss of the prudence principle and judgement of risk from accounting and auditing practices.

Vicky Ford puts forward a cogent case that it is not just bad regulations that need to be changed, but the very process from which they emerge – starting with the European Union's legislative process. Opaque regulatory processes that prevent post-hoc correction of unintended results and are vulnerable to capture by the special interests of governments and industries are destined to produce bad outcomes, she says. Jackman demands that we roll back the onset of tick-box rule-making and instate a simple but powerful system of regulation based on principles.

The age-old debate

Although our contributors are in broad agreement on the need for greater competition and customer choice, stronger ethics, and better regulation, there is – unsurprisingly – less consensus about how these goals will be achieved. Perhaps this is related to a fundamental difference of view among about the design and regulation of markets.

On one side of the argument are those looking to usher in a pure and functioning free market where market forces push the industry towards where consumers think it should be. Thus far, consumer inertia, high barriers to entry, the too-big-to-fail problem, and other issues have conspired against a free and efficient market, so perhaps market forces could create a better system.

Those on the other side of the argument believe an effective market is a pre-condition for a better banking system but that market forces are not enough. Through mandated frameworks – codes of practice for example – the pro-regulation camp want to set co-ordinates for where the banking industry *should* be and then set rules aimed at guiding it towards that destination. Many authors argue that because banking is an essential utility, regulation is required to ensure universal access and that the economy can reach its full potential.

It's certainly true that the nature of banking products can be complex, and the informational advantage held by providers can allow the unscrupulous and the incompetent to survive and thrive however competitive the environment. Indeed, fierce competitive pressures might even exacerbate consumer exploitation. If you've had a bad haircut, you know it instantly and you don't go back next time. But how many purchasers of personal indemnity insurance could tell that what they were buying was overpriced, of poor quality, and often unnecessary? Given what some bankers get up to when no one is looking, is a more hands-off environment really a good idea?

On the other hand, regulation is undoubtedly prone to 'unintended consequences' which can cause more trouble than it ever tried to address. This seems nowhere more evident than in the banking industry. Capital adequacy rules, for example, make it far more expensive for a bank to lend to a Greek restaurant in London than to buy Greek government bonds – which are deemed an entirely 'risk-free' purchase by the Basel Committee. Regulators can become too big and too powerful but simultaneously too easily gamed. Democracy can be subverted by unaccountable or captured regulation that overrides the aggregate daily choices of millions of empowered consumers. Rules can undermine the ability of firms to grow, and stifle the ability of firms to innovate and improve customer service. Can we trust regulators to get it right (this time)?

All this mirrors centuries of political debate on the boundaries of market and state, so it is not surprising to see it reflected in the different stances of our authors. To attempt to resolve this debate here would be wildly ambitious. This said, in this collection of essays there seems to us to be a remarkable level of agreement across the political spectrum on several themes, and universal agreement that there is plenty more work to do.

Where to next?

There are three further areas, touched on by some of our contributors, that we feel have not been adequately debated during the course of current reforms.

First, the fundamental question of what the banking system is actually *for*, including the social and environmental outcomes we might expect it to support. This is currently inaudible in the reform debate which seems to consider only what banking *does* – and it is notable that only Jackson and Thurso address it head-on in their essays. This lack of public discussion means that even if there is consensus on the purpose of banking – which we suggest there is not – it remains hidden and non-negotiable. There may be broad agreement that banking (to evoke Lord Turner's well-turned phrase) should be 'socially useful', but we see little reason to believe there is consensus about what this means, or how we might know whether it has been achieved.

Second, there seems to be a lack of appreciation of the implications of fractional reserve banking. Baker considers the importance of banks' ability to create new bank deposits when they make loans; although this fact is clearly stated by central bankers, it is not well understood amongst policymakers or the public. As a result its significance has been lost: if banks create the money supply, can we really consider banking reform in isolation of monetary reform?

Finally, Mann, Kamell, Garnier, and Baker, to varying degrees, all show a willingness to question what was, until the recent banking crisis in Cyprus, a holy cow of modern banking: the sanctity of the general public's bank deposits. At its heart, this is about aligning risk and reward – surely a central tenet of capitalism. As Kamall points out, the hubris of bankers and regulators thinking that risk had been engineered out of existence by ever more complex financial models and instruments was a large factor in the financial crisis. Baker exposes the intellectual flaw of promising that instantly available and utterly safe bank deposits can be backed by long-term risky credit – an alchemy achieved only by state guarantees of deposits. This creates moral hazard for depositors and bank executives alike, both of whom are sheltered from the consequences of their choices and actions.

Conclusion

Where does this leave our vision of banking in 2020? We have some ideas for the future. But, as several contributors point out, delivering change might not be easy. Banks have resisted the reform agenda. In the interests of political point-scoring and swelling the competitive advantage of their countries over others, politicians prone to game-playing undermine the integrity of serious international work towards getting the rules right.

On questions of competition, choice, ethics, and regulation we see progress beyond what is currently in the pipeline, but in broadly the same direction. Beyond this we also perceive a more radical and intriguing space. Will we delve deeper into the political economy of what a socially useful banking system means, and whether competition is a sufficient condition to achieve it? Will we conclude that the ability to earn a return on money without taking any risks is fundamentally at odds with the principles of capitalism, and usher in an era where depositors can choose between 'safety deposit' bank accounts for which they pay a fee, and 'investment' bank accounts on which they earn a return at the risk of bearing a potential loss? Will we even question the very underlying basis of the modern fractional reserve banking system and ask ourselves not just 'Where does money come from?' but rather 'How *should* money be created and by whom?'

These questions might seem esoteric and less immediately useful than the essential practical steps on competition, choice, ethics, and regulation outlined in these essays. Furthermore, bank executives, policymakers, and the public alike would be forgiven for being weary of the subject of banking reform and for yearning to talk about something else. That is fair enough; but as Kramer argues, we must resist the temptation to relax when good economic times return. It is not enough to merely patch up the banking system so it poses less of a danger to itself and the public than it did in 2008. The UK wants and deserves the best possible banking system, and this might be a journey rather than a destination. We hope that this collection of essays helps point us a little further down the road to a better banking future, because if there's one thing we can all agree on, it is that a better future for Britain depends on it.

MAKING CURRENT ACCOUNT SWITCHING WORK

Andrea Leadsom

Why competition in the banking industry is important

One of the most significant crises in modern business is the decline of trust in the banking industry and in wider financial services. Small businesses are finding credit hard to come by, taxpayers are livid at the billions spent on bailouts, products have been mis-sold and indicators manipulated, pay for bankers is too often unrelated to performance, and customer service levels are often poor.

One of the most striking aspects of the financial crisis, and more recent scandals, such as Libor rigging, was the lack of choice that ordinary people felt when faced with a tableau of institutional failure. Much has been made of the regulatory shortcomings that have contributed to these problems, and public opinion often reflects on the actions of government and regulators. However, little attention has been directed at the competitive environment itself. And a competitive market is one of the best ways of ensuring these problems are not repeated.

In 2000 there were 41 major British banking groups and subsidiaries; in 2010 there were just 22. Four banks account for almost 80% of the personal current account and small and medium enterprise (SME) lending markets. There is evidently a need for genuinely comprehensive action to increase competition in British banking.

The real, game-changing solution is full bank account number portability. If it were as easy for someone to switch current account provider as it now is to change mobile phone provider – i.e. without having to change their bank account details – I believe it would lead to a huge increase in competition and consumer choice and to the elimination of barriers to entry.

I am not alone. Support for the idea is growing. Chief Executive of the Royal Bank of Scotland (RBS) Stephen Hester has said publicly: 'RBS supports moves to improve, speed up and simplify current account switching for retail customers. There are important technical challenges but these should be treated as issues to constructively work through not insoluble blockers to the end goal. The principle should be that if a customer wants to leave or join us, unreasonable obstacles should not be put in their way.'

Executive Director for Financial Stability at the Bank of England, Andy Haldane, told the Treasury Select Committee in January that 'the bigger prize, however, is having a switch take place in a more seamless, costless and timely fashion all of the time, not just at the point of failure. Historically it has been the case that people have found it costly and time consuming to toggle between different current accounts. I think many of those costs are still true today and if those costs were lifted and freed up, that would be very healthy, in particular for the new entrants who suffer from the inertia that is embedded in the current system.'

The Treasury too, is genuinely warm to the idea. A consultation is underway on a new payments regulator, to be established under the Financial Services (Banking Reform) Bill, charged with ensuring equal, fair, and transparent access to payment systems such as Vocalink. In November, Treasury Financial Secretary Greg Clark indicated his support for bank account number portability: 'We need much more competition in the banking industry, and account portability can have a major role in advancing that.'

A 'game changer' for our financial services

As Adam Smith pointed out in *The Wealth of Nations*, a competitive environment requires 'free entry' and 'free exit' of market players. This has not been the situation with banking in this country for years. Much has already been done to reduce the regulatory barriers to entry, including recent improvements to bank licensing to allow new and small banks to operate under a less onerous regime. The successors to the Financial Services Authority (FSA) – the Prudential Regulation Authority and the Financial Conduct Authority – are each required to have an eye to promoting competition.

But to fundamentally change the competitive environment, we need to give new banks the chance to compete on a level playing field for retail business. That will only happen if customers can freely switch to them, and the banks can in turn freely access payments systems. That is why the government should demand that full account number portability is achieved within the next ten years. There would be wide-ranging benefits:

- Businesses and individuals could change bank accounts overnight, with no need to change account details unless they want to, thereby making it much easier and more attractive to customers to change provider.
- The possibility of overnight switching would result in much greater competition between banks, which would need to differentiate their offering and service levels in order to retain customers, rather than relying on inertia, as is now the case.
- Any newly authorised bank would be able to buy a licence to use the shared payments system, and could instantly attract new customers. This would be a boost to challenger banks and take away the unfair advantage enjoyed by long-established clearing banks.
- Accounts could be transferred overnight from failed institutions to sound ones which, set in the context of a future financial collapse or a potential run on a bank, is obviously an additional massive plus for full account number portability. This would obviate the potential need for a bailout, and provide the means for resolution in the event of failure.
- The payments infrastructure employed currently by the big clearing banks is no longer fit for purpose. As we saw recently with RBS IT failures, the billions a year being spent to patch up creaking payments infrastructure is akin to the money spent trying to maintain the Victorian sewers – in the end, we have to accept that the exponential rise in the number of users, and the age of the old system itself, means we need to think again.

- A shared payments system, regulated independently (rather than by the banks themselves, as is now the case), where all account numbers and payments instructions are held within the shared infrastructure (rather than by the banks) would mean each customer can directly access the most up-to-date mobile payments and cash management technology without relying on their bank 'permitting' access. Customers could maintain several accounts or just one, and could switch any or all of them temporarily or permanently. The regulator would make sure each bank held enough cash in the system to cover customer payments, and that switching levels on any given day did not risk a run on a bank.

Dispelling the myths

There are some, mainly the big banks themselves, who argue it's too complicated and too costly to implement and will lead to an unstable banking system. This is simply not the case:

1. The technology to implement full account number portability and to facilitate bank resolution already exists. Vocalink provides the payments infrastructure that currently carries out all payments. It is owned by the big banks, but the government has announced plans to consult on creating an independent payments regulator tasked with ensuring fair, transparent, and equal access. Vocalink could easily be the vehicle through which full account number portability can be achieved.

   Customers are already able to make payments using their mobile phone number and this is being rolled out nationally with the building of a central mobile phone number to a bank account database. Banks also complain that abolishing sort codes and 'starting again' would remove the pillar of the international remittances process. But in implementing full account number portability, solving the sort code issue could be as simple as a gradual migration to a central utility system which uses a 14-digit account number where the first six numbers are the old sort codes and are used for international transactions.

2. There is no evidence it will be costly. As the infrastructure to implement bank account number portability already exists, the forecast from banks that it will be prohibitively expensive to

implement is false. New research by Vocalink itself indicates it would *not* be prohibitively expensive to introduce a new system to enable instantaneous switching.

As the banks will need to renew systems anyway, it may be that a central utility is, in fact, far cheaper than individual new systems. The key to minimising costs is to have a strategic payment plan that allows banks' current IT investment plans to be focused on portability and account resolution so all parties know how investment will be split across banks and across the central utility.

3. An unstable banking system would not result from the establishment of a central utility. It is the case that if accounts could be switched at the touch of a button, a run on a bank might be more likely than at present. However, this is also the advantage of the system as accounts could be switched from a failing bank quickly and seamlessly without any problems for the customer.

   The real danger is a malicious or accidental run on a bank – also a concern with the seven-day switching system advocated by the Vickers Commission and currently being developed by the Payments Council – which would need to be guarded against. This could be done by regulation restricting the number of switches in any one day or, as in the case of shares in a stock exchange, the regulator stopping specific bank switching in certain circumstances.

   In the very worst case scenarios, as seen in Cyprus recently, where limits are placed on how much money customers can transfer and withdraw, regulatory measures can be taken to guard against an unstable system emerging.

Why seven-day switching is not enough

The seven-day switching service being introduced following the Vickers Report is a positive step but it is a point on the road and not the destination. The bottom line is that it is not the same, nor is it even similar to full bank account number portability.

Seven-day switching does not remove any of the 'administration' of switching accounts which is a burden for individual customers, SMEs, and public sector organisations. It will actually increase the administrative burden on SMEs as accounts can be switched more quickly and more easily and therefore potentially more often, meaning SMEs are faced with the burden of constantly changing customer bank account details. Full bank account number portability would remove the bureaucracy of account switching and remove the burden on SMEs because bank account numbers are unchanged.

Seven-day switching does not deal with the current competition barrier to new entrants; it does not promote challenger banks, neither does it address crumbling legacy systems. It is a 'string and sellotape' solution which does not and cannot deal with the oligopoly of the big banks and the problems faced by challenger banks and SMEs.

Only a game-changer like adopting full bank account number portability will show that banks are serious about change and about restoring their reputation with the public. The sad truth is that I very much doubt the big banks will sign up for number portability without being dragged to it through regulation. Turkeys don't normally vote for Christmas. The challenge is for government to see through the protestations and fix its gaze on the long-term gain for our economy and for this vitally important sector.

How we can achieve bank account number portability

Intellect, a trade body representing the UK technology industry, outlines how the system could work in its recent report *Biting the Bullet*. Payment mandate information such as direct debits, standing orders, and a unique customer identifier would be stored in a 'central utility'. Both account switching and mass account migration become a case of simply changing the specific target of the current account data rather than having to re-establish all of the mandates, such as direct debits and standing orders, associated with a customer's account.

Similarly, receivables directed to the customer's account, such as their salary, will not require alteration, as they will be referencing the unique customer identifier. They will therefore continue to function normally when the underlying target current account associated with the customer's unique identifier is switched to a new provider.

In effect, all account information relating to a specific individual or business will 'hang' from a unique identifier – in essence a portable number retained by that individual or business on an ongoing basis.

Conclusion

Full bank account number portability is an idea whose time has come.

It would be great for the customer and for challenger banks. It would also be good for established banks: they should have nothing to fear from it being easier for customers to switch. A sector which currently lies at rock bottom in public opinion would be able to thrive, responsibly, as it has not done for some time.

The Financial Services (Banking Reform) Bill is a unique opportunity to set the wheels in motion. It will be a tragedy if the Bill passes without a government amendment leading to full bank account number portability.

Now is not the time for timidity, nor is it the time for false economies. This is a policy objective which would enable power to remain with the market without undue intervention from regulators and legislators. This is a vision for the future of banking, and it is a vision that we could achieve within ten years.

BANKING THE UNBANKED

Andy Love

To not have an account is, by its very nature, a defining characteristic of financial exclusion. For those who remain trapped in the cash economy, with all the additional costs that result, access to a bank account is fast becoming an urgent priority. As a result, the strategy to deliver financial inclusion by 2020 must have at its core the objective of banking the unbanked.

According to the *Access to Financial Services* Treasury report, a bank account is 'an important foundation for putting low-income households in the position to manage their money effectively, securely and confidently'. Accounts also deliver the added benefit of acting as a gateway to other cost-effective financial services, including savings products, insurance, and credit

Basic Bank Accounts (BBAs) were specifically designed for those on low incomes. Since their introduction in 1999 it is estimated 8.4 million transactional BBAs have been opened, with the number growing by more than half a million every year. By 2008/2009, the number of people without a bank account had halved and the proportion of people living in unbanked households had fallen from 8% to 3%. Unfortunately, this early success has not been sustained and the number of unbanked has remained static since then.

Sustainability issues

This matters because in the decade or so since the introduction of the BBAs, access has become even more important. More and more consumer services rely on making and receiving direct payments. Employers are shifting away from using cash and cheques. Welfare payments require a budgeting account. All this adds significantly to the pressure on poorer households to open a bank account.

Recent research confirms the increase in BBAs comes predominantly from other consumer groups – for example, current account holders switching to BBAs and those with no credit rating who are offered a BBA as a consequence – rather than the unbanked target audience.

There are many reasons why the unbanked remain so. As the numbers of unbanked adults reduce, it is likely they have become concentrated amongst the most-excluded groups who are suspicious of banks and prefer to manage their finances in cash. Many are reluctant to engage as a result of a negative banking experience and there have been real difficulties in opening accounts as a result of banks insisting on forms of identity such as a passport (to comply with money laundering regulations) that some potential customers simply do not possess.

Yet even with the many barriers to entry, research for the Financial Inclusion Taskforce found a majority (52%) of the unbanked would definitely or probably like to open an account. The problem stems from the current model for personal current accounts. Under the 'free-if-in-credit' model, banks generate revenue in three different ways: from overdraft fees and interest, from net credit interest, and from interchange income from debit card use. Although it is possible to incur overdraft fees, in principle only the last two charges apply to BBAs. But they do not generate significant income as most BBA customers are unlikely to have a high-enough credit balance in their account. Additionally, the opportunities for cross-selling other, more profitable, products are limited, making the overall business case for the BBA more difficult to sustain.

Minimum standards for BBAs

The share of the BBA market varies considerably between banks. Statistics on penetration levels are no longer published, but from the available evidence it is not unreasonable to assume some banks are not pulling their weight. Whether a result of failure to promote the product or restrictions on access to branches, the net effect for an industry which considers the BBA uneconomic has been a 'race to the bottom' characterised by an erosion of many of the features of the BBA driven by the desire to cut costs. Recent evidence presented to the Parliamentary Committee on Banking Standards confirms this but also widespread recognition efforts must be made to counter this trend through the adoption of a set of minimum standards for the BBA. With only a very basic industry-wide standard defining the BBA as an account with no overdraft and no chequebook, the scope for the withdrawal of services remains significant.

What should those minimum standards be?
According to research commissioned by Consumer Focus, the main features that appeal to BBA holders and those inclined to open an account – the majority of the unbanked – are having a debit card followed by standing orders and access to the branch network. There is recognition by the banks that the functions of a BBA need to be brought up-to-date with technical developments and changes in the market. Some of the features currently under discussion include access to cash through the Link network, standing orders and direct debits, a debit card, and features to enable the account to remain in credit – but as yet there is little sign of an emerging consensus.

The other issue where agreement remains elusive is around access. Should all customers who want to open an account be able to do so? The banks claim to offer accounts to all customers apart from those posing legal risks such as fraud or money laundering – yet many with a legitimate right to open an account find it impossible. Many argue banks have a moral responsibility to help, but the industry counters that BBAs are not profitable and it is onerous and unfair to suggest they should be required to offer an expensive product to all customers.

Impacting the BBA market

With fundamental differences on minimum standards and availability, it is understandable many conclude nothing much will change. That would be a mistake. During the next few years, the combination of changing public attitudes, market developments, and regulatory change will have a significant impact on the BBA market.

First, there is the issue of self interest. The fact is that the public reputation of banks and bankers is at an all-time low. Considerable effort has been made to address the problem with, it has to be said, limited success. In the absence of a profit motive, the business case for a BBA becomes the reputational benefit of being seen to address the needs of the financially excluded. To achieve the maximum benefit, banks should explicitly brand the product and publicise its availability and features to the public.

Some will argue if banks do this collectively, then there will be no obvious reputational benefit for any individual bank. But this is a crisis of confidence in the banking industry as a whole and there is therefore a very strong argument that, if the industry takes steps to improve the service to its most vulnerable customers, it will have a positive impact on public attitude to the banking sector.

Secondly, the government is currently consulting on a fundamental reform of the payments system. Out goes self-regulation under the proposals, and in comes some form of payments utility regulator. Although there may be some delay before it is fully established, it is widely expected to deliver a benefit to consumers by exposing the true costs of the banking industry. For personal current accounts, including BBAs, this should be a priority, as it will recognise that virtually all the costs of the BBA are shared across a much wider, and more profitable, range of products.

The true cost for banks will be the incremental cost of the BBA. This is likely to be a fraction of the cost currently assumed, thus throwing into doubt the industry's claim that BBAs are 'costly and unfair'.

Thirdly, we now have a more active regulator empowered to deal with market failure on behalf of consumers. When exercising its new competition mandate, the newly established Financial Conduct

Authority 'may have regard' as to whether consumers in areas of social and economic deprivation can access and use financial services. While these powers have often been ignored by previous regulators, the FCA – with its remit to encourage competition for the benefit of consumers – will be under considerable pressure not to ignore the financial exclusion experienced by many vulnerable consumers. An early test of its powers will be whether or not it can challenge the race to the bottom.

Should industry inaction continue and the service to BBA customers deteriorate, there is every reason for regulatory intervention to follow.

Fourthly, competition will inevitably play a key role. Regulatory change will make it easier for new challenger banks to enter the market and compete on a level playing field. A limited bank account redirection service will reduce the barriers to switching banks and is likely to be superseded by full account portability to promote even greater competition. It is hoped this leads to a diversity of provision of bank accounts, with differing funding models to suit the needs of all of their customers, including the unbanked.

Finally, changes in the welfare state and the introduction of the Universal Credit (UC) make it increasingly likely that there will be a rising demand for a BBA in which to pay monthly benefits. Add to this the prospect of the withdrawal of the post office card account (POCA) with over 3 million, mainly elderly, customers and you have potentially the biggest challenge to our banking industry in a generation. Any agreement resulting from current discussions must recognise that achieving the objectives of the welfare state requires almost all of the unbanked to become banked.

What of those who are unwilling to open an account? Can they be won over by new innovative, low-cost, easy-to-manage, alternatives to traditional banking? Pre-paid cards have been suggested by some, but they are not able to offer transactional banking as cost-effectively as a BBA. Improved POCAs (if they are not scrapped) and the use of mobile phones to transfer funds are in their early stages. The reality is while a comprehensive bank network offering BBAs is available to the public, the incentive for other providers to innovate in that space is greatly reduced. Of course, innovation in mobile telephony and card technology will reap some benefits for the consumer. But to those resistant to banking, neither of these options is likely to replace the BBA as a cheap and secure – and for the vast majority of those consumers entering banking, the preferred – method of managing their finances.

Meeting the needs of the unbanked

How will the changes outlined deliver banking services that meet the needs of the unbanked? The pressure to deliver higher standards and better customer service to the traditionally unbanked will require recognition that access to a BBA must be open to all, excepting only those who pose a risk of some form of illegal activity. Greater transparency about the true cost of banking services will ensure customers are treated fairly, help drive down costs, and improve services to the traditionally unbanked. In the absence of the profit motive, we have seen that competition between banks can lead to a race to the bottom. Agreement on minimum standards is the way to meet this challenge. Regulatory pressure on costs and services should minimise the difference between mainstream accounts and BBAs, with the retention of those features that are attractive to the unbanked such as no overdraft and no cheque book.

The combination of government action, regulatory activism, and market pressure will do much to improve and extend the BBA market by 2020. But the banks must also play their part. They must each make a public commitment to the provision of a transactional account to anyone who asks. These accounts should have broadly the same features as mainstream ones, but with modest variations to meet particular needs. The charging framework must reflect the costs of providing those banking services to the customer.

For those who argue the cost will be onerous and unfair, the reality is that it is a small price to pay for an industry that desperately needs to restore its reputation with the public. Banking the unbanked will provide one tangible step towards that goal.

PUTTING THE CUSTOMER AT THE HEART OF BANKING

Chris Leslie

If you want to decide which of the various bank scandals of the last five years is the most systemically important, then there is a broad range from which to choose. From the appalling high-risk decisions taken by hubristic traders, to the mis-selling of financial products to small businesses around the country, banks have made a series of dodgy and dangerous decisions which have been to the detriment of their customers.

Years after the onset of the crisis, however, it was the revelation of widespread attempts to rig the Libor rate that triggered a fresh wave of public revulsion. The apparent joy with which traders sought to pull the wool over people's eyes – complete with rewards of Bollinger and nicknames like 'big boy' – convinced the public, not just that the attitude of individual banks to risk and reward needed to change, but that the whole culture needed reform.

George Osborne has come up with a plan but – just as with his all-too-casual efforts to stimulate growth – he has not gone far enough. In the spring he presented the Financial Services (Banking Reform) Bill, a half-finished set of proposals to be rushed through the House of Commons even as Andrew Tyrie's Commission on Banking Standards is still going about its work.

What is missing is a series of reforms on vital issues like rebuilding consumer choice, boosting financial inclusion, and creating a more diverse marketplace.

In omitting these areas, and in choosing to water down the recommendations made by Sir John Vickers, who rightly concluded structural firewalls are needed to supplement capital safety buffers, the Chancellor has passed up a chance to draw a line in the sand for a troubled industry.

Customer service at the heart of the banking culture

So, instead it has fallen to Labour try to complete this half-finished Bill; to ensure radical reform of the culture and standards of banking and to give consumers greater choice in a market which has for too long been dominated by a handful of players.

Labour's vision for banking in 2020 is an industry with customer service at the heart of its culture and a system requiring bankers to give an undertaking to act ethically and legally. A new diverse banking system would increase choice on the high-street, empower Britons to move their accounts to get a better service, and rebuild the relationship between branches and local customers. The reformed system would not exploit but rather help those consumers in need of financial education.

Earlier this year Labour tabled a series of amendments to the Financial Services (Banking Reform) Bill to try to bring about such a shift in culture. The government resisted these at virtually every opportunity, which risked sending the message to the City that it is business as usual, despite the creation of the ring-fence.

The standards of behaviour at individual banks and among their staff are, however, vital to what might be called the post-Vickers landscape. If the right tone is set in the boardroom, it will be reflected on the trading floor. If the attitude is wrong, then the deals done will be dangerous. As the Salz review of Barclays made clear, there is a direct link between a bank's levels of pay, bonuses, and culture and its attitude towards the rules.

'We could not avoid concluding that pay contributed significantly to a sense among a few that they were somehow unaffected by the ordinary rules,' wrote Anthony Salz.

'The institutional cleverness . . . stretched relationships with regulators and resulted in them and the market questioning some of

Barclays' financial information. Barclays was sometimes perceived as being within the letter of the law but not within its spirit.'

Such a culture must not, and should not, be seen again. All of Britain's Big Five banks are scarred by scandals of ethics or competence and all have changed their management since the start of the financial crisis. The time is now ripe for creating a new model of banking and Labour is playing its part.

A vision for the future

Central to Labour's vision of a reformed industry is the establishment of a system of licensing under which bankers must operate. If doctors can be struck off, after a fair hearing, when they have acted corruptly or incompetently, then there is no reason why we should not apply the same standards to people who are dealing with millions or even billions of pounds of customers' money. Risks to the nation's economic health need to be taken just as seriously as risks to individuals' personal health.

A new licensing regime would restore confidence in our banking system, both for British consumers and for international clients and investors.

It is true that controlled functions (those with greater significance) can currently only be carried out by 'approved persons', and that there is a 'fit and proper test' that must be passed. However, this clearly has not worked and has not prevented our banks from being run like casinos. The failure of individuals to live up to fit and proper standards can be shown by one simple figure – the near-£20 billion paid out by the Big Five banks last year in fines and compensation for mis-selling.

This number illustrates the extent to which bankers rode roughshod over the approved persons' regime. Now they must be held to account. A bankers' licence should be a formal requirement and would bring the financial services industry into line with doctors and parts of the professional services industry, such as the law.

A licensing regime should be accompanied by a code of conduct spelling out exactly what is required of people working in the City. A code was recommended by The Future of Banking Commission, a cross-party body including Vince Cable, David Davis, and Lord McFall, set up by Which? in 2010.

This type of code would form a major part of the drive to raise regulatory standards and restore consumer confidence. By making bankers sign a document, it would also concentrate their minds on the fact that breaking the rules would put their jobs and salaries at risk.

Fiduciary duty

A good banker will always treat a client's money as their own – striving to deliver a decent return without taking on huge risks. This sense of safeguarding someone else's money, known in law as fiduciary duty, needs to be embedded in the bricks as we rebuild the City of London. There is a long way to go before public confidence is restored and it is no surprise that nearly two-thirds of banking customers no longer trust their lender to look after their money, according to a YouGov poll for *The Sunday Times* last year.

Such a deficit of trust makes it all the more remarkable, then, that the government has consistently resisted our attempts to create a fiduciary duty, giving a legal obligation of banks to act in the best interest of customers. We want to give consumers confidence that companies selling financial services products are acting in a prudent and ethical manner.

Labour's amendment, tabled at committee stage of the Financial Services (Banking Reform) Bill, would have required a ring-fenced body not to act contrary to their customers' interests while carrying out core activities. It would also have had the broader effect of giving financial services professionals a responsibility to act reasonably when dealing with customers, brought these duties within the remit of the regulator and ensured the forest of paperwork supplied to consumers is balanced by the need for clear and consistent information.

If these are the ways to reform bankers' behaviour, then just as much thought and effort is required if we are to open up the market to new entrants, boost choice for consumers, and ensure basic services are provided to all Britons, regardless of how much they earn or where they live. After years of dominance by the biggest banks, this will not be an easy task, but there are several key areas in which modest reforms can significantly improve fairness and increase access to finance.

Making the banking sector more competitive

One of the most important of these is the need for a review of the competitiveness of the sector. The Big Five banks consistently score below average in Which? customer satisfaction surveys yet the majority of Britons have never switched their main personal current account. So we need to expand choice by clearing the obstacles to setting up new banks. The Vickers Report is clear that even after the limited divestments by Lloyds and the Royal Bank of Scotland (RBS), major retail banking markets will still be more concentrated than at the time of the Cruickshank Report into competition 13 years ago.

The Bank of England and the now-defunct Financial Services Authority (FSA) have announced new measures, such as lower capital requirements and a quicker authorisation process, to make it easier to open a challenger bank and for new banks to find investors. We think change has to go further, however, particularly as RBS has still not signed a deal to sell the 318 branches which must be divested under EU state aid rules. This is why we have called on the Treasury to carry out a review into all the barriers to entry to high street banking.

If there are more banks in Britain, they will all have to create incentives to switch account providers by offering a better deal. Consumers are currently put off from switching by the difficulty of moving their standing orders and wages or salaries to a new institution. Remarkably, the average person is more likely to get divorced than to change their current account provider. The government's chosen means to tackle this problem – an industry-led seven-day redirection service – is feeble and unambitious. We want full account portability, which must surely be considered as an idea whose time is rapidly approaching.

This, along with expanding the right to a Basic Bank Account (BBA), would ensure a better deal for consumers. A BBA is defined as one with a debit or ATM card but not an overdraft function, interest on deposits, or periodic fees. Credit is a necessity for so many people if, for example, they need to bridge the gap between paydays – but BBA facilities have begun to be chipped away at and some high street banks have pulled out of the Link cash machine network. Ensuring access to an account is a vital part of tackling financial exclusion, and will take us forward in preventing some poor or disadvantaged people from falling into the clutches of unscrupulous payday lenders.

There are already many credible alternatives to payday lenders and we must to do more to promote the work of community finance development institutions (CDFIs). One way to do this is for banks to publish local lending data in an anonymous form and broken down by postcode. In the USA, the publication of business lending data was written into law after it won support from President Obama.

British banks should have an obligation to offer loans and other products in every community around the country. If they are not prepared to do so themselves, then they should do so through CDFIs, charity banks, or credit unions.

This is what a one nation banking system will look like. It is an industry in which bankers act responsibly, in which lenders don't use jargon and a mountain of paperwork to exploit their clients, and in which consumers have a genuine choice of providers when they walk down their high street. It is one in which the Big Five compete with smaller banks and new entrants to provide the best service. And one in which our historic mutual sector – which was forgotten about despite the pledges made in the Coalition Agreement – is a major part of the market for savers and house buyers.

PUTTING ETHICS BACK INTO BANKING

David Jackman

Banking is not incompatible with ethics, even though some find it easier to suggest this is so. Shareholder primacy and 'the free market' have become convenient excuses for greed. This undignified departure into a detached, insulated, even deified, parallel financial universe is all our faults, and it serves us poorly. How can banking do better?

We need practical policy steps, set within a credible and engaging social and economic narrative.

First, regulation has to intervene more robustly. It has to deliver outcomes instead of simply carrying out prescribed processes. Regulators feel safer designing a 'good process' rather than having to think about the point of what they are doing. The endless application of business rules has, already, spectacularly failed to prevent pensions and payment protection insurance (PPI) mis-selling. How many banks did the Basel capital requirements save in 2008? Instead, regulators need to address directly the crucial things which determine how banks behave: their values, cultures, ethics, incentives, and results.

This requires answers about the role of banking and the outcomes we desire as its starting point. A discussion of the social purpose of banking, gamefully kicked off by Financial Services Authority (FSA) Chair, Lord Turner, shortly after the crash, was typically and speedily misinterpreted and driven into the sand by banks and their house-trained lobbyists, for fear the answer might threaten the sanctity of bonuses. With the introduction of ring-fencing, we now can at least make some distinction between the character and needs of institutional and consumer-facing business. However, the apparently opposing faces of this coin are of the same currency and any intervention needs to handle heavy-weight conflicts of interest.

The only way of dealing with such muscular tensions is to brace regulation along a skeleton of tough principles that work internationally and bind to the toughest sinews of social justice and sustainable progress. The body of banking – and, indeed, capital itself – is, and must be, held aloft by an energy to nurture and grow other forms of human endeavour including robust and resilient communities, social enterprise, intergenerational equity, and the alleviation of poverty. These are worthy pursuits for all parts of a banking system which relies unashamedly on ethics for a sense of direction.

A values-led practice

I first published *An Ethical Framework for Financial Services* at the FSA in 2002. Setting out core values derived within a framework of developing maturity across the sector, it is worth reading again. The maturity espoused requires the constant ferment and challenge of ethics and principles, to continually redefine and remake a shared picture of outcomes. I have termed this 'values-led' practice.

This is not a flaccid, light-touch version of regulatory capture; far from it. This is hitting banks with subjects they cannot duck, on issues we all understand, with rules that cannot be gamed or subverted: fitness and properness, lying and deceit, fairness and care, competence and good governance. These are matters compliance traditionally finds difficult and the FSA only dabbled with initiatives such as 'Treating Customers Fairly' (TCF). I have witnessed systemic squirming and desperate clutching at tick-box mechanical systems and controls to take away the pain of thinking. Unfortunately for managers, 'doing ethics' is hardly a one-hour 'sheep-dip' training session.

Regulators should not pander to such displacement activity. They need reprogramming or reselecting to demand proper standards in:

- Independence
- Governance
- Effective challenge
- Competence and integrity
- Community engagement and accountability
- Sustainability

Such a compliance 'crunch' should not hurt banks or drive them away. If they have the quality of imagination and the calibre of people, principle-based regulation can increase prosperity not hinder it. It just requires a much more directed effort and fewer feckless and lazy avoidance strategies. Recent research carried out by Resources Global Professionals and the University of Edinburgh Business School for a Resources Governance Index looking at different sectors and jurisdictions shows a definite correlation between good (mature) governance and long-term return on assets.

Return and ownership

This moves the argument onto the twin drivers of return and ownership. We are living with the legacy of Companies Acts, whose antecedents come from an age when it was necessary to re-assure investors in far-off railway schemes and empire-building trading companies that they would one day get something back. Shareholders take risks; there is no reason nowadays for their risks to have priority over other stakeholders. Why not equalise their claims with communities, customers (not the same thing), employees (to some extent), and wider economies? Companies could then make much more sophisticated, balanced, and mature judgements about strategy and how they distribute returns based on the same core principles and outcomes sketched out for regulators. A convergence of objectives is entirely possible if the rigidities in international company law we have inherited can be modernised.

Who does own the banks? A specific policy statement could be to differentiate between responsible ownership and general share holding. Surely a computer trading programme that holds shares for nanoseconds is not an owner? Voting rights could be reserved for a class of shareholder who retains their shares for a sustained period – say three years. This would encourage an orientation of corporate concern towards those who had a real, practical interest in the long-term success of the company and its sustainability. This would have some impact in stemming the short-termism that cripples responsible investment. It would also allow the bonus 'problem' to be re-cast by measures of long-term value creation.

Taking improvements to the community as a useful unit of receiving and evaluating long-term value generation, how measurement of community value-added might work in practice is set out in a new and pioneering sustainable and resilient communities standard (BS8904) from the British Standards Institute, the sustainable communities committee which I chair. This is now being elevated to an international framework (ISO 37150). These use a development or maturity matrix to allow for complex and outcome-focused metrics. This elegant model of community healthiness and capacity building is well placed to form a core of any broad, just, and progressive socio-economic narrative.

Beyond regulatory and company law reform

Capital rarely really understands this language of ethics and outcome. Banks might have community investment departments, partnership reports, and a bevy of sustainability gongs; but these rarely inform the everyday behaviour of the boardroom, the engine rooms of trading floors, call centres, or high street branches. So, how is it possible to break into the cosy bubble of big banks beyond regulatory and company law reform?

One policy answer is to cut international banking adrift – along the lines of the ring-fence – and wait for reforms to come from the inevitably politicised but growing pressure for international regulation, and then to concentrate on retail ethics through encouraging a new stratum of lending provider. In this space, are we not placing too much hope in the camp of new challenger banks who may offer more of the same if in miniature, or the mutual sector which has already pretty much sold its soul in an effort to ape its big brother's characteristics (and pay)?

Instead, perhaps an option is offered by the model of credit unions which are based on constructs of mutuality and common bond. In Ireland, for example, half the population has credit union accounts and this has kept the real-time economy ticking over while the big banks have imploded, or so grievously let down their society as to have no credibility.

Credit unions offer what people need – loans at decent rates and budget accounts to manage limited resources. They do not desire to be 'flash' or 'racy' or driven by shareholder pressures. They are based on a common bond of shared interest, respect, and self-help. They simply look after your money and offer an increasing range of practical services that do not need massive capital balances or international reach. Yes they need to professionalise more and in Ireland there are strenuous efforts underway to rationalise the 410 unions into more effective groups, but there is no desire (nor should there be) to lose touch with their community roots, their local accountability, and their duty of care.

The UK does have a weakly developed credit union sector but it tends to be reserved to distressed inner-city communities. Serious tax incentives for taking part in active 'membership' of an institution (rather than it competing on price or interest rates) could dramatically boost traction. It is possible to envisage a far more proactive and widespread credit union movement based on perfectly adequate and proportionate legislation and regulation already in place. The Community Interest Company (CIC) corporate structure, once championed by Gordon Brown, could provide the architecture for even more grassroots engagement in financial self-help operating as local tentacles of a credit union hub.

All of this suggests a more deeply rooted and diversified retail structure beneath the current big banks which would serve everyday financial needs, potentially increase financial inclusion, almost certainly raise levels of public financial literacy, and have the added benefit of encouraging or forcing some degree of adjustment in a bank's own level of service and ethics.

The process of challenge and engagement

This general approach speaks to a wider social narrative of co-operative action based on ethical principles that are constantly reworked as openly as possible and capture the learning from our own experience as much as that of previous generations. Socially inclusive principles have been formulated into a new charter for the twenty-first century, the Grasmere Charter, written by myself and Reverend Cameron Butland. How the process of challenge and engagement could work in a wider democratic, community-based, context is set out in a new paper I wrote with Richard Lemmey called *Plan 'C'*.

We rely too much on the placebo of regulation. Having lived through one complete cycle of financial regulation, from the first self-regulatory organisations of the early 1990s to the consolidation represented by the formation of FSA in 1998, to the twin peak approach which has just come into force, I am fairly sure history will repeat itself and we will be looking for a single regulator by 2020. The twin peaks system will struggle because there is no longer one institution balancing tensions between practitioners and service users. A regulator using half an ethical framework is only likely to come up with a half-decent conclusion. That conclusion, once cemented into a rulebook, will be permanently at odds with a conclusion based on a set of principles which is in turn based on an opposing position and set on partial interests. The current structure is motivated by political vindictiveness and a desire for a fresh start. It is unlikely, on past form, to last ten years. And we would be better served by a more difficult but integrated system.

Banking at the retail level should be designed to serve the everyday financial needs of most of us: safe-keeping, saving, small loans, mortgages, insurance, and credit. The aim is to help us manage our cash flow, to make provision for the future, and to help small businesses form and grow. This is a community concern. The rest is a different game – high-net-worth services for a few and commercial banking demands international reserves of capital and international regulation. Both can be knitted together by ethics-based principles in which the UK can take the lead, but for the next phase we have to wait for other centres such as the USA and Germany to catch up – and they will. Singapore has an interesting role here because it stands to gain from any tightening of controls in the UK as some business migrates east. But, at the same time it wants to demonstrate its position and credentials as the responsible leader in Asia – and it has a deep understanding of the value of good governance. Does it hold off acting to potentially gain from any arbitrage or does Singapore join the UK in driving up global standards? It is about critical mass and momentum and the momentum is already building.

A NEW APPROACH TO INVESTMENT BANKING

John Mann

The best place to go is Glasgow's Ibrox stadium. There you will see the consequences of toxic debt. A product that people want to buy; a product that expands too quickly through easy money and is strangled by the debt burden. But no bank sank Glasgow Rangers. The banks have been happy to keep toxic debt moving around the system. And we have let them.

When I sat facing Bob Diamond in the Treasury Select Committee hearing on Libor manipulation, I couldn't help feeling even after being forced to resign and hauled in front of Parliament to give evidence, that he was wholly unaccountable. He remained untouchable. He out-lawyered the government and out-blanked every politician. He demonstrated just how far we haven't come in fixing the flaws in our financial system. If ever there was a poster-boy for financial reform, I think Bob Diamond would be it.

What I can't reconcile is, where are the courageous leaders, the ones fighting for the reforms we desperately need? Why is nobody willing to lose some friends in order to clean up this mess?

My reaction to the Treasury's plans in the Financial Services (Banking Reform) Bill is to ask: 'Is this it?' Considering what we have been through and the problems in British and world banking, is this Bill the best that we, as legislators, can do? If that is the case, it is no surprise we are increasingly derided outside the walls of Westminster.

As Kenneth Rogoff – Professor of Economics at Harvard University – has observed: 'Financial regulation isn't fixed, it's just more complicated. Little has fundamentally changed since the 2008 financial crisis.'

In order to create a banking system England can rely on and be proud of, we must be ambitious, innovative, willing to learn from our neighbours, and unafraid of making enemies. My vision of what British banking could be involves a system with a reputation for reliability, not risk; for care, not corruption; and for moderation, not manipulation.

The pillars of reform are straightforward. If enacted properly, they will result in a system we wouldn't recognise today. We must accept – or rather champion – the decline of the investment bank. We must step up our fight for stronger and simpler regulation, be better engaged in the European debate where many of the rules are set, and continue our battle to radically change the culture in our banks. We must get the financial system to do what it's supposed to do: provide the infrastructure for financing and lending on which our economy is built. And, crucially, we must be uncompromising in our expectation of transparency, both in terms of tax havens and how consumers are put at financial risk by the banking industry.

Investment banking

The government has set out its plans to split retail and investment banking. Separating the two branches of banking through a 'ring-fence' will make banks more resilient, and ensure it is easier to resolve problems in the event of future failure. However, the deadline set in the Bill for implementation should be 2014 rather than 2019 and the split should be complete, not simply a ring-fence. The success of this decision is well documented; in the United States, the passage of the Glass-Steagall Act of 1933 – a document of just 37 pages – helped produce financial stability for the greater part of seven decades. That's almost two years of security for every page of regulation. It is not as complicated as it looks.

What differentiates the UK is the extremity of the its reliance on investment banking, unlike in particular Germany and China. What can these two resilient and growing economies teach us about innovation in the banking system?

Whilst we are sellotaping over the banking system, China is building a competitive base that will dominate world economies for decades. China uses a model of cheap finance, concentration on raw materials and technological transfer, investment in skills and infrastructure, and medium-term planning. China shows how ruthless simplicity creates permanent competitive advantage, in contrast to short-termism creating momentary advantage. We play with paper; it builds with concrete, developing tomorrow's building technology along the way.

In Germany, banking is harnessed and put to work pulling the community forward instead of taking it for a ride. The government-owned development bank KfW was formed in 1948 as part of the Marshall Plan as a central loan corporation. By the 1970s KfW was making frequent use of the capital market. It was able to use the revenues generated from non-concessional loans to support its rapidly growing domestic promotion programmes – which it still does to this day.

However, KfW has no branches and does not deal directly with the ultimate borrower for its domestic business. In order to receive funding, customers apply to their own, private bank for financing. This application is forwarded to KfW which then assesses the project against its key strategic targets to promote small and medium enterprises (SMEs), clean technology, nationally important infrastructure projects, and international project finance.

KfW is a signatory to the UN PRI – Principles for Responsible Investments – and acts as an SRI – Socially Responsible Investor. Accordingly, it invests almost exclusively in bonds from issuers who comply with high environmental, social and governance standards. It is, for want of a better phrase, an ethical bank.

Despite the onset of the financial crisis, the KfW Special Programme managed to secure sufficient credit for SMEs – nearly 5000 applications for €13.3 billion were approved by the end of 2009. The programme also had a positive impact on employment, securing over 1.2 million jobs.

KfW's capital comes from the German government. It issues bonds that are unconditionally guaranteed by the government and finances

90% of its borrowing. From a relatively small base of just €3 billion paid-in capital and €13 billion 'callable' capital, KfW has outstanding borrowing of €445 billion and, and at the end of 2011, had a loan portfolio of €495 billion. Total new lending in 2011 was €70.4 billion.

Because its borrowings are guaranteed by the German state, it enjoys the same credit rating as that Government and hence similarly low borrowing costs. This – together with its exemption from corporation tax and certain regulatory requirements of the German Banking Act, and the fact that its equity is unremunerated – means it is able to channel lending at a lower interest rate and over a longer time period than would be obtainable on the private market. The structure is a good example of how a government's credit rating and financial capacity can be harnessed to lever substantial amounts of lending, and support government-defined policy objectives, from a very small direct commitment of funds. And yet we seem to have taken no notice.

In the UK, companies can in fact access lending – this is not the key problem. The real issue is the cost of lending which is much higher to businesses in the UK than in competing economies. Instead of talking about the Bank of England base rate, we should be quoting the real cost of lending – just like with Libor, we seem to favour non-existent indicators. A new national investment bank could lend money at affordable rates. Low confidence and the high cost of money are the issues stifling economic recovery.

Stronger and simpler regulation

A simpler and more transparent system of regulation will ultimately lead to greater stability for our economy. For two decades, finance has been getting incrementally more complicated. Neither regulators, politicians, nor many of the banks have been able to keep up. Financial institutions ran risks they did not understand; investors could not oversee the management of their own assets; and regulators were not sufficiently knowledgeable to fulfil their role as overseers. Complication led to confusion, which led to crisis.

In order to ensure this never happens again, we must overhaul our entire regulatory architecture. We must make certain the authorities have the tools and the power they need to deliver effective regulation; we must re-imagine the role of the compliance departments, and have banks demonstrate publicly how they are meeting new codes of practice.

With much financial regulation originating in Brussels, the Prime Minister must appoint someone in his cabinet who camps out in Europe, not just to follow decisions but to author the document up for discussion. We are increasingly ceding our invisibles sector to Frankfurt and Paris, immobilised by fear of change and paranoia of European engagement. In ten years we will be bit players unless we alter our paradigm of engagement very soon. Neither the government nor the Labour opposition has anything informative to say on reforming the Eurozone, an issue set to determine European financial systems for the foreseeable future. Outside Europe we are easy prey for international speculators, doomed to years of Japanese-style economic anguish. Time is running out.

We must go much further to tackle excessive remuneration in the banking sector. Remuneration should be linked to risk. Risk must be taken in the right areas. More women in banking must help reset testosterone levels and help make long-term corporate planning more valued. Each bank must employ a standards officer with full data access rights and a legally defined role of upholding the bank's agreed standards of propriety and behaviour, both set by the bank and required by regulators. Compliance officers must have a new degree-level professional qualification. There must be criminal sanctions at board level, including for non-executive directors for failure to act properly in financial matters.

Getting serious about transparency

We need to spread risk, transparently, through the introduction of a system of tiered risk and return for consumers. The idea we can guarantee every type of saving for ever up to a certain limit – £85,000, or whatever it ends up being in the future – is irrational. I would like a real choice between low interest rates and total security for my money, and medium or higher risk: a 'standard' bank account with no risk or interest to depositors and a full taxpayer guarantee; an 'investment' account with some risk, some return to depositors but with a lesser government guarantee on savings; a 'high investment' accounts with higher risk, potentially higher returns but no government guarantee. Similar tiered risks should be introduced on other financial products with any implied government guarantees, such as ISAs. We should give the consumer the choice rather than pretend the state will always be able to provide a bailout.

As well as transparency on the risks faced by people using bank accounts, I want to see transparency when it comes to tax. There has been a lot of talk about tax havens. The government claims it is serious about clamping down on corporate tax avoidance and going after tax dodgers at home. But when it comes to banking, the biggest loophole involves the UK Crown dependencies. We have a significant degree of influence over them and they rely on us for their legal system and their defence, but we allow them to facilitate opaqueness in finance, whether banking, commercial, personal, or a combination thereof. No wonder my file is full of cases of money laundering and other criminal corruption that have been found out, and those are only the ones people have been able to see. That opaqueness should go, and we have the power to do it. If the government is really serious about dealing with tax avoidance, it should sign transparency and anti-tax-avoidance agreements with every UK Crown dependency by 2015.

Conclusion

The system I have set before you is the only way for Britain to remain a successful global financial centre without asking the country to continue to bear unacceptable risks. Such wholesale change will not cause us to lose our competitive edge internationally, as argued by those who benefit from the status quo; rather it will enhance our reputation with investors, depositors, and borrowers everywhere.

Unless we act now, we will become a second-tier economy, living on the glories of the recent past; history perhaps repeating itself, but this time the competition is from the Premier league.

An economy run by bankers will leave the UK as the Sheffield Wednesday of the football world. Once glorious. Sometimes entertaining. Loved and loyal. But not able to shake off the ghosts of finances past. This is the nation's choice.

GETTING RETAIL AND INVESTMENT BANKING RIGHT

John Thurso

On the basis that those who do not learn from history are doomed to repeat it, the next systemic banking collapse is due in 2088, give or take a few years. Between then and now there will be a few runs and probably the odd bank will collapse. Approximately every 80 years or so there has been a systemic collapse of some kind in banking. The causes are remarkably similar, as indeed seem to be the proposed remedies. At their heart are cheap credit, an asset bubble, poor lending, and a failure to assess risk. The remedy is a massive support operation by the central bank and government, followed by legislation and a tightening of regulation. Most importantly, for a couple of generations, the institutional memory of bankers imbues sufficient caution to act against most excessive risk. Yet, over time the memory fades and the tragedy, or farce, repeats itself.

Beyond making money

Policymakers and legislators are once again busy seeking solutions. Most of this work is around structure. Nirvana is a system allowing an orderly failure of individual banks in a manner that protects citizens and the payments system and minimises the implicit guarantee from the state.

Only time will tell whether this attempt proves any better than previous attempts, or whether it survives the temptation of future generations to repeal legislation. However, all of these activities ignore the most fundamental question. Banks clearly have a role beyond making money for shareholders. By common consent banking is essential to individuals and to commerce. How much of what they do is therefore an activity that goes beyond simple profit and has a particular value to society? To what extent are some banking activities pure profit-making without any societal value? In short what are banks for?

For the moment the world has broadly accepted capitalism as its system of choice. The ownership of assets by individuals, the right to private property, and the ability of individuals to create businesses and wealth, as well as to lose it, are now accepted pretty well universally. It does not mean this is right, but it does put a unique responsibility on banks and the banking system as the guardians of accumulated wealth and the providers of capital for enterprise to ensure the system's safety and efficiency. The first decade of the twenty-first century can be categorised as having allocated capital in a particularly wasteful and inefficient manner. This distortion has not only undermined the general economy but it has had a profound effect on society by misallocating capital away from the common good and towards some individuals with whom it delivered no discernible societal gain. The future of the banking system must therefore, above all else, be able to fulfil its wider remit to society of an effective and beneficial use of capital.

Banks are unique in that they each provide a service that is indispensable to their customers, and it is the customers who are taking the risk in doing business with the bank. There are many commercial endeavours where the industry as a whole is vital: food production, energy supply, construction, communications, and transportation to name but a few. However, as sporadic collapses such as Enron and WorldComm have demonstrated, individual enterprises can go under without any systemic impact, notwithstanding individual tragedy for employees and customers. By contrast, the collapse of a bank nearly always has systemic implications requiring a resolution procedure quite separate to straightforward insolvency. In addition, the exposure of the customer to the non-bank failure is reasonably survivable. By contrast, the failure of a bank without protection almost inevitably results in many, if not most, customers facing terminal financial difficulty.

Until recently banks could be identified quite simply as deposit-taking institutions that operated a payment system, and provided current accounts and credit to individuals or businesses. This 'utility' function remains the core of any high-street bank. It is the part legislation is designed to protect and the part which, if it fails, causes runs and crises.

Merchant or investment banks do not, as a rule, hold deposits but instead act to facilitate raising capital for companies, governments, and individuals combined with advice and deal-making. Some include market-making activities, although many market-making activities take place outside the banking system. Today's 'universal' bank combines all three activities in one business.

Societal benefit

Whilst the utility aspect of banking has obvious value, the distinction between the utility and the rest of banking activities as 'casino' actually masks the important role played by those institutions that facilitate raising capital both as intermediaries between those who have capital and those who need it, and as advisors assisting businesses to grow and create wealth. This is as necessary an activity as running a payments system. Market-making has the least obvious utility value. It is perfectly possible to conceive a system where all capital instruments are sold by banks on a peer-to-peer (P2P) or even peer-to-individual basis, with the market for such instruments being conducted by others for whom it is their sole business. In particular in those areas where the market-maker is effectively acting as a bookmaker, and where the market is a zero-sum game, it is hard to accord any particular value other than expediency. A major defect of modern banking is the amount of capital, created by lending, and then consumed by trading which produces negligible societal benefit, as opposed to investment in wealth creation which does.

If a future vision of banking is of a system that first provides the utility (safe deposits, a secure payments system, and prudent commercial credit) and benefits society through capital allocation that helps to create overall wealth and economic growth, then our legislation and regulation must be shaped with that vision as its primary objective. The utility protection will come, as much as it ever can, from the structural changes flowing from the Vickers Commission. But questions about capital allocation are as much cultural as regulatory. So legislation has to be framed accordingly; recognising the importance of different cultures and allowing them to flourish in the right place is crucial.

The first step is to recognise that small specialists are rarely systemically threatening and to shape regulation so that the larger an institution becomes – and the more systemic risk it therefore poses – the greater the regulatory burden it bears. It must also be recognised that the more financial risk is borne individually and therefore directly connected to individual reward, the more individuals will seek to manage that risk effectively. The only reason institutions such as Goldman Sachs turned themselves from partnerships into companies is that there was no advantage in remaining a partnership, as the risks could be laid off from the old owners (the partners) to the new owners (the stockholders) whilst the rewards could be maintained. It is not possible to reverse that procedure for large institutions, but it should be possible for new entrants through a combination of regulation and tax treatment to become unlimited liability partnerships and to benefit from the rewards whilst also taking more account of the consequences of risk.

The second step is to recognise that different kinds of banking activity have, and should have, a different culture. This should be reinforced in the training, remuneration, and values of each activity. Thus the high-street banker should be a reasonably prudent individual, primarily involved in long-term relations with their customers, looking after their money and providing for their credit needs in a sensible way. They should be respected members of the community who understand the responsibilities of looking after people and their money and act accordingly. The values will be about service and judgement. The remuneration will reflect the importance of the role but variable pay will be a relatively small part of the overall package.

The relationship between the investment banker and their client is of equal importance but founded on a different matrix. Whether raising capital or undertaking Mergers and Acquisitions activity, the client risk appetite is greater and they are well advised: here the job of the banker is to help them fulfil that requirement. The risk appetite is greater, as is the potential for failure, and therefore the cost, both to the client and to the institution. It is therefore right that the culture, values, and remuneration accord with the difference in activity and risk appetite.

The universal bank requires special attention. The utility and investment cultures can co-exist in different segments of an organisation, but it is essential that retail culture always prevails at the top. At board level, variable remuneration has failed to align reward with the long-term sustainability of the institution and has clearly increased appetite for risk. It is far better to pay a salary recognising the responsibilities of office, with only modest bonus potential, to ensure correct respect for future risk.

The third step is to realign reward in the capital allocation system away from debt instruments and back towards equity. One of the most interesting comparisons between the SME financing landscape in America and in the UK is the relative ease with which American SMEs can access capital through equity. In the UK by contrast, it is typically bank debt and retained earnings which deliver future investment. One side effect is that well-run small and medium enterprises (SMEs) will hoard cash in a downturn as they know from bitter experience that bank assistance is always counter-cyclical – available in boom times and absent in downturns. Following a trading recession, banks return to easing credit reasonably quickly; however, following financial recessions banks take much longer to ease credit conditions causing an ongoing brake on recovery. If, however, banks acted either as principal or agent in securing a better balance of equity finance for SMEs, then some of this cyclicality could be removed and a better allocation of capital achieved.

The final step is to create much greater plurality. Banking in the UK is dominated by a relatively small number of very large players. Compared to the landscape in the 1990s when finance was available from a wider range of domestic banks, as well as an array of mutuals, the average business is likely to have a bare choice of a few providers in any given area. Further, it is clear all banks operate a broadly similar model to broadly similar criteria. Thus, in a banking downturn, there is no effective competition. The first remedy is to make conditions for new entrants easier, recognising that smaller-scale institutions do not carry nationally systemic risks.

The second is to look at the existing players through a competition prism and use the national investment in banking to help create a more diverse landscape.

Banking: A socially useful activity

The true failure of the banking system that ultimately led to the crash of 2008 was not simply that it indulged in all the classic activities that have led to every other banking crisis in history, but rather because, perhaps more than ever before, it lost complete touch with the value of banking to society – or indeed with the concept that it should have such a value. Like a struck-off doctor or a defrocked vicar, disgraced bankers have damaged the institution of banking as much as they have damaged themselves. Those now left to rebuild must not only ensure banks are reasonably safe and resolvable when stressed but that they are a trusted place to put deposits, get advice, and secure a mortgage. They must also make sure their use of capital, our capital, is for the benefit of society through wealth creation overall and that it is not, as it was in the past decade, used by a small number of individuals to create personal wealth.

However, achieving this also requires policymakers to set aside the desire for retribution and instead create conditions through regulation and taxation which steer banking back to a socially useful activity. Before that can be done, we need to know banking will respond positively to the challenge. In the short term, the government should use the holdings in the nationalised banks, particularly the Royal Bank of Scotland (RBS), to make a cultural change. As it would be difficult for this to happen with RBS weighed down by debt, separation into a good and bad bank is essential. A real opportunity for change would come from causing a cultural shift with RBS as a leader rather than a follower.

If, therefore, the vision is of banks at the heart of commerce and industry helping sustainable wealth creation and societal growth, with personal wealth creation a by-product rather than the central goal, then a cultural change is an absolute requirement. Where better for the government to start the process than in its own bank?

GETTING SMEs THE FINANCE THEY NEED

Mark Garnier

In an R5 Live interview not so long ago, a business owner in Bristol complained his bank would only lend him money for expansion if he was prepared to put up a personal guarantee. 'Why,' he asked, 'does my bank not believe in my business?' The answer, of course, was because he did not believe in his business himself. By refusing to put up a personal guarantee, he sent a clear message to his bank he was uncertain of his plan's prospects.

Similarly, a Midlands-based small printer was recently seeking around £15,000 to upgrade his computers. He was prepared to put up his £150,000 printing machine as collateral against the loan – a not insignificant proposal on his part as this is his business's single most valuable asset. But the bank told him it was unable to accept the printer as the asset for an asset-backed finance scheme and so couldn't help. 'But,' it said, 'we can lend you up to £20,000 for a car up to eight years old if you fancy that instead.' Whether this was a tacit way of saying they would lend against the business owner's Jaguar instead is still out for debate, but the key point was missed by the business owner: if the loan was called in against the printer, not only was the printer a tricky piece of kit to realise its asset value, it also meant the business was no longer viable and so all other loans were likely to fall over as well.

Access to finance

The small and medium enterprise (SME) sector is one of the most varied and important, but it is also one of the most fragile. Lacking the critical mass and resources of some of their larger peers, SMEs can be more susceptible to economic changes. SMEs highlight economic uncertainty, lack of consumer demand, and fuel costs as three of the four areas of concern for the future. The fourth barrier SMEs cite is access to finance.

My vision for the future of banking is one where businesses can get efficient access to finance and the help offered to them by myriad government schemes. Banks will, of course, try to help businesses understand their requirements to secure loans and advances, and business organisations also provide some help on this point. But, SMEs are a key driver of growth in the UK and their efficient funding is vital to the sector supporting economic recovery. To achieve this we need a banking system which understands business and a business world that is not put off looking for finance.

Currently, the picture on SME lending is unclear. Whilst (in its Voice of Small Business Index Q1 2013) the Federation of Small Businesses (FSB) highlights business loan rates coming down, just 41% of those surveyed were successful in applying for a loan with another 17% waiting for a decision. Indeed, just 20% of those surveyed had made an application for credit. The British Bankers' Association (BBA), however, reports that typically around 9% of SMEs will have made an application for a loan in the last year.

However, whilst the FSB indicates that nearly half of SMEs applying for credit are unsuccessful, the BBA claims that 71% of businesses are successful in new or renewed loan applications. Indeed, bank chiefs, when asked, will claim that as many as 85% of loan applications are granted.

The truth is there are a number of factors at play. At the most basic level, an SME owner or manager may see the bad headlines and simply not bother to seek finance in the belief that they will be rejected. This is reinforced by the fact some businesses believe a rejection somehow registers on a credit score for the business. This is further compounded by the fact that banks do not necessarily treat a loan enquiry as a formal application and many no-hopers are rejected before a formal application is made, explaining some of the difference between the FSB and BBA surveys.

Mismatched expectations

Crucial to much of the problem is a lack of understanding between the bank and the business manager of what each other does and what each other expects.

Banks, at their most basic level, are simple. They are merely a balance sheet with customers attached to both sides. A customer - depositor - lends money to the bank and in so doing appears as a liability. The bank then seeks to gain a return on the money it has borrowed by lending it out at a higher rate than it has paid the depositor, and that loan to a borrower appears as an asset. The simplicity of this example is important: for a bank to function in any meaningful way as a bank, it has to lend money.

But, the very act of lending money is a risk. The depositor, notwithstanding the government guarantee of £85,000 for deposits, is at risk of the bank being unable to pay back the loan. In order for the bank to be able to secure deposits, it has to demonstrate that it is lending prudently - even more so now that the banking and regulatory reform is keen to ensure the taxpayer will not stand behind the banks in any future crises.

Despite this, in lending to a business, the bank is writing what amounts to a call option. In the event of a successful loan to a business, the bank wins by getting back what it has loaned plus the agreed rate of interest; but the shareholders of the business win the increase in the value of their equity as a result of the successful use of gearing - a significantly higher return than the bank. Should the business fail, the bank loses its loan and its interest. The business owner loses their equity, of course, but their upside is significantly greater than the bank's, whilst the downside is the same. So the bank has to align the owner's risk with the bank's risk, and assess all the risks to the loan (economic, skills resource of the business, opportunity, etc.). It is at this point that the mismatch of expectations starts to become apparent, as the stories at the start of this essay demonstrate.

Problems faced

There are other problems banks face outside of those influenced by businesses. The reforms after the banking crises put more pressure on banks to shrink their balance sheets and, with one of the crises banks – the Royal Bank of Scotland (RBS) – holding a significant share of the SME lending market, there is inevitably pressure on the overall picture. Add to that the Basel III requirements, being delivered through CRD IV, that weigh SME lending as the highest level of risk with regard to risk weightings and the pressure is on for SMEs seeking loan financing.

It is no wonder around a third of SMEs do not use formal methods of external financing at all, relying on retained earnings or personal finance to fund investment and growth. The rest, who do seek external finance, are almost entirely reliant on the banks. Just 2% of SMEs use external equity as a source of finance. The Dragon's Den, it seems, has not yet sunk into the general psyche of SMEs.

One of the issues against equity financing, aside from the perception by a business owner that they will be reducing their control of the business, is that the cost of debt financing carries favourable tax benefits. This in itself creates a perverse incentive that could be reversed through alternative methods of tax treatment of the cost of equity finance.

To help counter the headwinds against SME lending, the government has, since 1981, put in place a series of debt-guarantee schemes of various shapes and sizes, from the Small Firms Loans Guarantee Scheme to the Enterprise Finance Guarantee in 2009. But, irrespective of who guarantees the loan, and therefore the cost to the SME of the loan, the bank still has to process the application. Cheap loans are often accompanied by expensive set-up charges.

Possible solutions

There are a number of solutions in place. The current government has provided support for businesses through a number of schemes. But whilst these are admirable in their intention, the sheer number of them (10) can make things confusing: Enterprise Finance Guarantee, Enterprise Capital Funds, Business Angel Co-Investment Fund, Business Finance Partnership, Seed Enterprise Investment Scheme, National Loan Guarantee Scheme, Community Investment Tax Relief, Tackling Late Payment / Promoting Prompt Payment, National Loan Guarantee Scheme, and the

Growth Accelerator offer a bewildering array of opportunities for businesses.

The Local Enterprise Partnerships provide a service for businesses to access advice, but the problem still remains: average business owners find themselves in a very lonely place, more often than not unaware of the options available to them largely as a result of not being a member of any professional body, such as the FSB.

Despite an array of alternative providers of finance, such as peer-to-peer (P2P) lenders and community investment funds, banks dominate the market place in terms of size and brand recognition and are the first stop for a vast majority of businesses seeking finance. Because of this, some argue banks should be seen as utilities and there is a great deal of support for nationalised banks – RBS especially – to be broken up. This is the right course of action. It should be broken into two parts with one part providing a depository for bad loans, to clear the banking system of bad forbearance, currently under the radar as a result of cheap financing costs; and the second part providing a state-owned utility bank that is a one-stop shop offering a full range of government and commercially driven initiatives and advice for all businesses, especially SMEs and micro businesses.

But whilst a state-owned bank (run on a commercial basis), within the confines of the proposed ring-fence under the Financial Services (Banking Reform) Bill, could be a very efficient quick fix solution, for it to be able to develop a better SME support culture, the 'New RBS' must be open to significant competition.

It is vital that an efficient banking market opens up for SMEs. The Financial Services Authority started the process of allowing easier access for new entrant banks and this should be continued by its successors – the Financial Conduct Authority and the Prudential Regulation Authority – with their approvals process. It should certainly be the case that it is not prohibitively expensive to merely open the door for negotiations with the regulator. Importantly, greater competition would lead to greater choice, not just with a plethora of banks offering the same product, but with banks offering specialist funding services.

A typical bank seeking to help a local specialist business will still need to go through the process of understanding that customer's business model: a specialist bank will already understand it, driving down the cost of funding applications for that type of business. We are a maritime nation, yet there is still no specialist marine financer amongst the UK banking sector.

The government runs the risk of trying to solve problems with yet another initiative. This would not be a solution, merely an extra ingredient to confuse the already over-flavoured offering. A business friendly, state-owned utility bank operating in an environment of increased competition through a simpler banking licence approval process and a more lenient regulatory requirement for early start-up banks will drive banks to better utilise their existing strongest asset: their distribution network. This will allow not just more, transparent banks, but also a wider variety of bank types – including alternative providers such as P2P lenders and community investment schemes.

Finally, education. Education comes in many forms and getting information out to businesses is the simplest. As the government regularly contacts businesses for a wide variety of tax and regulation-related reasons, it seems a simple ask for government to use these opportunities to tell businesses what is available, and to encourage businesses to seek help from professional organisations and Local Enterprise Partnerships.

But there has been a big educational deficit up to now, i.e failing to realise that financial education should be part of the curriculum. That is now changing and that is a good thing, but it will take a generation for our new entrepreneurs to be entirely comfortable with finance and money management as a result.

It is from this basis of education – whether through schools or other routes – that we can, as a society, drive a step change in financing options for businesses: a step change that sees business leaders seeing equity investment as a proper and sensible alternative to debt financing. For a challenger bank, the opportunity to offer equity finance (whether as principal or broker) through its existing distribution network offers, possibly, one of the greatest transformational changes to SME financing for the future.

GOING WITH THE CROWD

Sharon Bowles and Damian Horton

At the time of writing much is afoot in the EU. The text of the Capital Requirements Directive and Regulation (CRD4), implementing Basel lll, has just been agreed. It is one of the legs meant to make banking safer with better quality and higher capital buffers. Another of the legs, recovery and resolution planning, which includes details of how to have bail-in-able bonds, is under discussion.

The Eurozone Troika's rescue remedy for Cyprus is a real-life demonstration of what happens to depositors in fractional reserve banking when there is not a sufficient cushion of bondholders, equity, or other capital. 'Too poor to bail out' is the new 'too big to fail'. There may be unique problems in Europe because of the still-evolving Euro project, but the lessons of the need for adequately capitalised banks are for everyone. So, too, is the need to have clear processes for allocating losses and unwinding complex financial intermediation. When we think about potential future bank structures we need to remember these key facts: they should be designed to withstand the unknown and have limited incentive to break or arbitrage a set of rules.

Adapting, improving, and innovating

Some templates for the future of banking have been set out, including ring-fencing of retail and investment arms. A great deal of movement has already begun in the development of new and alternative retail banks. The bigger challenge is adapting, improving, and innovating around investment banks and methods of capital allocation.

Investment banking, portrayed as 'casino' banking by many, has a very important role to play in our economies. Investors, including pension funds, need to be financially connected to companies. This financial intermediation – creating and trading financial assets – is important for allocating capital to people, entrepreneurs, and businesses that are likely to be profitable and beneficial to society.

So a key part of capitalism is having institutions that move money around. The simplest form can be through lending, also performed by retail banks; to larger global companies this can be through bond issuance, securitisation, or equity issuance. Derivatives – complex financial instruments based on other financial instruments – are another format of capital allocation and grew in popularity due to the belief that they optimised asset allocation and increased financial liquidity, which is the availability and flow of capital. The result is a highly complex system that can be efficient yet has risks of systematic shock, as experienced after the collapse of Lehman Brothers.

With the growth of larger corporations and the development of financial processes, we now have pension funds and insurance companies as well as banks allocating capital. Despite seeming diverse, the chain of intermediation has become both long and too reliant on correlation (statistics designed to show how securities move in relation to each other). This is because when looking at assets in a long chain of intermediation, reliance on numerical measures or indicators, along with multiple points of diversification, becomes dominant over knowing a business. Hence regulation has a reliance on those numerical measures, including credit ratings, to the extent that the simply 'knowing the business' is squeezed out.

The European Parliament tried to blow some life back into relationship lending in CRD4 but met the brick wall of 'how is that to be defined and checked'. The fact is that it cannot be done by tick boxes; looking forward perhaps we should rename it 'knowledge lending'. This is also where it becomes evident that vocational and ethical training is needed in finance as well as manufacturing.

Easy trading

Following on from the financial crisis we have a lot more concentration on liquidity within regulation, and in general this presses towards trading and the easily tradable rather than locked-in investment. Easy trading – particularly when it comes to debt instruments – also means more complexity and in fact more consumption of costs within the financial system. Such costs may boost bank turnover and GDP, but it is the area where one can ask: is it actually doing anything useful, or worse, is it restraining the useful?

For easy trading, bonds are made more liquid by the derivatives that surround them, which renders a simple investment more complex, and which of course is also encouraged by regulation. Long-dated bond purchases will be hedged with a futures contract to look after the short side, and indeed receive a regulatory reward for hedging. Meanwhile, those buying shorter-dated bonds will hedge the long side with a futures contract and get their regulatory reward, too. In the middle of these futures transactions, which will be netted off from one another, are the banks, obviously charging for their services.

The result of all this is that the bond investment chain is not short or simple and in the end trading takes place with derivatives rather than the investments themselves. And when a derivative has more liquidity than the underlying assets – and it is actively taught that this is a principle of some derivatives – we need to worry. The derivatives themselves are draining away the liquidity the underlying assets would experience if they were the only investment option. Similar regulatory encouragement to complexity applies in other asset classes and again, in the end, the trade ends up in the derivatives and not the underlying financial instrument itself.

Facing the future

Capitalism and banking needs to be about the process of providing capital, not the fancy formats of accounting laws. At present, too much human capital is wasted in finding tax or accounting arbitrages or discovering the price of complex methods of financial intermediation, human capital that would better serve the economy if applied to identifying and funding smarter and better technologies.

Of course, we cannot just abandon procedures we are used to but there is a link between progressive reduction of complexity and finding the right place to face the future. There are some weapons – a simple leverage ratio is one and transparency another – which are already on their way to being included. However, it is not enough just to add these; the aim must be to take away, too. One further simple measure is to remove the regulatory 'technical compliance' comfort blanket, prohibit multiple disclaimers, and leave those dealing in complexity exposed to its legal liabilities and consequences.

A more radical move, which could be done in parallel with existing banking, might be to promote models that simplify the investment chain with fewer intermediaries, fewer derivatives, and maybe even fewer asset classes. We will only know if, for example, a decentralised shorter system is better if it competes in parallel with our current one. However, simpler new models should not be tied down with the same regulatory complexity devised for complex systems; they should have appropriate enabling regulation.

Crowd funding is one method recently introduced. It will be part of the future and it should be embraced, not dismissed as fragmentation. Growing crowd funding safely is one of the challenges.

Crowd funding

Generation Y, the under-35s, has been badly shut out by the financial system and is carrying a disproportionate burden of the cures imposed post-crisis: asset price inflation and quantitative easing undermine their futures and they are moving to reject current ways. They want information now, on the web, and they want to understand more directly what they are getting into. So as investors they are likely to want more direct access to parts of the business they are interested in and can understand, and crowd funding may also provide a route to better distribution of wealth.

Capital allocation could be looked at in a different way: instead of herding asset classes with regulatory sheepdogs, we should question whether we might have gone up the wrong mountain with these sheep in the first place.

Where can we get to if we start with crowd funding? In this new phenomenon, businesses stick their idea up on a website, thereby using internet marketplace technology already developed by the likes of eBay. But crowd funding misses a number of key things: the public does not usually have either the skill or the time to pick individual investments which means there is still a need for financial experts, such as fund managers and executives, in order to build global companies and strategies. Crowd funding, in its current format, where it is completely decentralised, does not have the structure to build the global businesses needed in a globalised world and would fall short of competing with the existing system. And what we need is greater competition with a backbone.

A way to take the alternative banking model using crowd funding forward is to build larger companies from local subsidiaries, then fund these subsidiaries through crowd funding. In essence, franchises usually work this way; for example, with a local fast food chain owner using a bank loan to start a shop under licence. There is no reason why this cannot be either crowd funded or directly financed in other ways, instead of a bank loan at the local level. Indeed, one can also see similarities to worker-owned co-operatives where capital is brought in from employees, which is another way of collecting capital directly from people. There is similarity even in the existing process for larger companies issuing corporate bonds across a syndicate of banks, which can be broken down to steps of investment managers being shown the bonds, the funds buying the bonds, and also seeking investment from people. It is possible to skip some of the steps, and costs, in this latter process by turning it around. Thus local subsidiaries could be set up and linked in a 'reverse franchise' operation.

It is also possible to set up funds dedicated to investing in parts of a business alongside crowd funders – in effect a fund of franchises. The fund route suits those who have neither the time nor the expertise to invest, while the crowd-funding route suits those who want to get involved directly. Expanding further, it can also be a mechanism for existing fund holders, such as pensions and insurance companies, to deploy funds directly into the economy and have greater preference where their capital is allocated, something that might even assist the development of green technology.

Ultimate outsourcing

So, is the proposition that businesses should be franchises? Well, yes, or at least more of them should develop through or switch to this kind of funding model. But not in the same way that existing conglomerate franchises occur as they source a great deal of capital at the holding company level. Instead, capital should be mostly held locally, sourced in small parts, using the vehicles of crowd-funding and a fund. This franchising would need to be fuller, including non-core business functions such as HR and accounting – in other words: ultimate outsourcing.

What we have here then is the opportunity for a smart hedge fund or portfolio manager to become a pure investor. The emphasis on price discovery goes, but great investors will build up a fund of franchises by picking the best investments and returning superior profits. We would not waste the best human capital on price discovery; instead it gives smart people the opportunity to build a co-operative of operating businesses – an op-co co-op – as a founding block of a future bank model.

Is this manageable? Well part of the art is using natural management: this allows local subsidiaries to default, safely, even using this as motivation for local improvement and, for the larger entity, a form of self-repair. If local owners have to perform to survive and make profits, shared locally, then improvements will continually be sought by them rather than forced on businesses by top-down decisions.

This model changes the 'them-and-us' society of a banking elite and investors, or of executives and workers. Instead, with bottom-up capital sourcing and control, capital is closer to workers and to where real technological innovation is driven. It also adjusts capital structure into a decentralised form and spreads profits outwards, rather then centrally collecting them.

Conclusion

There have been massive technological advances and social networking is changing the way information is handled. There is already discussion about decentralised organisational structures; why should banking and investment not be touched by these changes, too? It is perhaps easier to see how the model would thrive in a developing country – they have leapt directly to mobile phone banking ahead of developed countries. But it ticks many boxes, from the lament of fund managers seeking returns and investment directly into the economy to the contempt for, and cost of, 'casino banking' activity.

This is one option for the future of banking. It is important to realise investment banks have useful purposes and a transition to more local retail banks may prevent the creation of new, global businesses needed for a very competitive world economy. We have a great deal of educational barriers to overcome, which includes modifying and improving concepts and models. The additional challenge is convincing people to allocate capital in new and innovative ways that are likely to benefit us all.

BANK REFORM DEMANDS MONETARY REFORM

Steve Baker

The complex and technical subject of bank reform has scarcely been more popular. Events in Cyprus have demonstrated banks are a way of investing money for a return, with all the risk that entails. Van and minibus entrepreneur Dave Fishwick has created a documentary – *Bank of Dave* – which shows banking can be a simple entrepreneurial function providing a safe return to savers at the entrepreneur's risk. It's award-winning and a soar-away popular success.

Of course, thanks to regulators, it's not actually a bank: it's a savings and loans firm. Whereas these route savings to borrowers, a bank creates credit. That is, banks lend money into existence.

It is that distinction, together with other features of the financial system, which has led the world into crisis. It is both one of the least well-understood economic phenomena of our time and the most central to our present difficulties. Yet, astonishingly, Dave Fishwick has struck on a model of banking close to a theoretical ideal: he carries his own commercial risks and, even if he could take deposits, he wouldn't provide credit in excess of savings.

It is towards this model the world should move.

The features of today's banking system

As Governor of the Bank of England Sir Mervyn King told us in 2010: 'Of all the many ways of organising banking, the worst is the one we have today.'

Notes and coins are irredeemable: the promise to pay the bearer on demand cannot be fulfilled, except with another note or coin with the same face value. Notes and coins are tokens worth less than their face value and are issued lawfully and exclusively by the state. This is fiat money.

When this money is deposited at the bank it becomes the bank's property and a liability. The bank does not retain a full reserve on demand deposits. In the days of gold as money, fractional reserves on demand deposits explained how banks created credit. Today, credit expansion is not bounded by the redemption of notes, coins, and bank deposits in gold.

Because banks are funded by demand deposits but create credit on longer terms, they are risky investment vehicles subject to runs in a loss of confidence. States have come to provide taxpayer-funded deposit insurance. This subsidises commercial risk, producing more of it and creating moral hazard amongst depositors who need not concern themselves with the conduct of banks.

The state also provides a privileged lender of last resort: the central bank. It lends to illiquid but solvent banks getting them through moments of crisis. In a fiat money system, central banks have the power to create reserves and otherwise intervene openly in the money markets. Today this is most evident in the purchase of government bonds with new money, so-called quantitative easing.

The central banks also manipulate interest rates in the hope of maintaining a particular rate of price inflation through just the right rate of credit expansion to match economic growth. That otherwise free-market economists and commentators support such obvious economic central planning is one of the absurdities of contemporary life.

Compounding these flaws is the limited liability corporate form. Whereas limited liability was introduced to protect stockholders from rapacious directors, its consequence today is ensuring no one taking commercial risks within banks stands to share in the downside. This creates further moral hazard.

Regulatory decisions have been taken to encourage banks to make bad loans and dispose of them irresponsibly. Among these are the

US Community Reinvestment Act and the present government's various initiatives to promote the housing market and further credit expansion.

Having insisted banks make bad loans, the regulatory state imposed the counterproductive International Financial Reporting Standards (IFRS) which can over-value assets and over-state the capital position of banks. This drives the creation of financial products and deals which appear profitable but which are actually loss-making. Since these notoriously involve vast quantities of instruments tied to default, the system is booby-trapped.

Amongst the many practical consequences of these policies was the tripling of the money supply (M4) in the UK from £700 billion in 1997 to £2.2 trillion in 2010. Credit expansion at this rate has had predictable and profound consequences including asset bubbles, sectoral and geographic imbalances, unjust wealth inequality, erosion of physical capital, excess consumption over saving, and the redirection of scarce resources into unsustainable uses.

Moreover, credit cannot be expanded without limit. Eventually, the real world catches up with credit not backed by tangible assets: booms are followed by busts.

Objectives for monetary reform

This crisis first emerged in banking. We were then told it was a debt crisis. Shortly, it will be generally realised that most money is created as debt and therefore this is a monetary crisis. Bank reform will then properly become a matter of monetary reform. Any plan for bank reform must therefore also be a plan for monetary reconstruction.

The goals of reform must include:

- The privatisation of commercial risks which are now socialised.
- The availability of bank accounts which provide safekeeping of money.
- Choice in currency.
- Prudent accounting rules.

- An end to systematic intervention in credit markets by central banks.

The following two proposals would deliver a free market in money and banking. Their authors differ passionately over the status of demand deposits but, in the end, they take two routes to systems whose differences are largely semantic. The merits of each proposal differ according to the circumstances and political realities in which reform becomes possible.

Constitutional fiat money as a route to free banking

Proposals for banking based on constitutional fiat money run in the tradition of Peel's 1844 Bank Charter Act and Irving Fisher's *100% Money*, published in 1935 and recently raised to prominence by the IMF.[1] The essence of the proposal is to separate the monetary and credit functions of the banking system by requiring a 100% reserve for demand deposits. Under such a system, bank runs are impossible, banks cannot create money, and a major source of business cycles is reduced or eliminated. Current accounts effectively become vaults for safekeeping and banks provide credit by intermediating between savers and borrowers.

A robust, comprehensive, and consistent justification of full-reserve banking from legal and economic principles is provided in Jesús Huerta de Soto's treatise, *Money, Bank Credit and Economic Cycles*. Controversially, he argues that it is a fraud to hold less than a 100% reserve against demand deposits of money, one with profoundly damaging consequences.

He identifies five stages in a process of reform, including central bank independence. The next and crucial steps for the UK may be summarised as follows:

Reform is announced: bank depositors decide to what extent they wish to swap their deposits for shares in the investment funds to be created.

By legislative act, every bank deposit becomes the property of the depositor, redeemable in cash produced by the state.

1 "The Chicago Plan Revisited", Jaromir Benes and Michael Kumhof, IMF WP/12/202

Having removed the banks' liability to depositors, the equivalent assets are placed in investment funds. Shares are issued proportionately to relevant depositors. The remaining shares are exchanged for outstanding government debt and other state liabilities, converted into bonds.

At this point, banks are safe: bank credit must be backed by savings and demand deposits are fully reserved under clear contractual principles. Savings would not be under taxpayer guarantee but could be privately guaranteed for competitive advantage. Investment funds would provide for those seeking short-term returns. Money supply growth would be transparently in the hands of the central bank: currency debasement to fund public spending would be clearly understood as such.

Huerta de Soto's plan is not inflationary. Changing the status of demand deposits and pledging to redeem them in cash does not create new money. Expropriating those assets of the banks acquired through decades of state-sponsored credit expansion could clear the state's debts and provide for at least a substantial proportion of future liabilities to the public.

In the remaining stages of his proposal, Huerta de Soto sets out steps to abolish the central bank and to provide for commodity money and free choice in currency. Ultimately, he provides for complete freedom in money and banking subject to a 100% reserve on demand deposits.

Finally, after the reform, the monetary and fiscal environment would demand honest politics. Former Federal Reserve Chairman Alan Greenspan concisely explained why in his essay *Gold and Economic Freedom*. He wrote:

> *Under a gold standard, the amount of credit that an economy can support is determined by the economy's tangible assets, since every credit instrument is ultimately a claim on some tangible asset. But government bonds are not backed by tangible wealth, only by the government's promise to pay out of future tax revenues, and cannot easily be absorbed by the financial markets. A large volume of new government bonds can be sold to the public only at progressively higher interest rates. Thus, government*

> *deficit spending under a gold standard is severely limited. The abandonment of the gold standard made it possible for the welfare statists to use the banking system as a means to an unlimited expansion of credit.*

That is why for 40 years our monetary arrangements have been not merely tolerated but encouraged: chronic credit expansion has facilitated the deficit spending necessary to support welfare states in excess of the tax base. This is the source of the debt crisis now engulfing mankind. A new, honest, and sustainable politics would be required by the new financial environment. This proposal provides that environment and a fiscal reset.

Moving directly to free banking
After the Huerta de Soto plan was published in 1998, credit expansion in the UK proceeded at an astounding pace, with the broad money supply more than tripling between 1997 and 2010. This produced various asset bubbles and other distortions in the structure of relative prices. The effect on banks has been worsened by imprudent IFRS accounting. It is therefore an open question whether bank assets are susceptible to Huerta de Soto's proposal.

An alternative route to deliver a free banking system without passing through constitutional fiat money has been brought forward, drawing on the work of Kevin Dowd and Richard Salsman, in an article for the Cobden Centre by Anthony J Evans. Under the title *2 days, 2 weeks, 2 months: A proposal for sound money,* the plan proceeds as follows:

Over two days – ensure all operating banks are solvent:

- Deposit insurance is removed – banks will not be able to rely on government support to gain the public's confidence.
- The Bank of England closes its discount window, which currently helps banks insure against liquidity shocks.
- Any company can freely enter the UK banking industry.
- Banks will be able to merge and consolidate as desired.

- Bankruptcy proceedings will be undertaken on all insolvent banks: suspend withdrawals to prevent a run; ensure deposits up to £50,000 are ring-fenced; write down bank's assets; perform a debt-for-equity swap on remaining deposits.
- Re-open with an exemption on capital gains tax to avoid unjust taxation on the new shares held by depositors.

Over two weeks – monitor the emergence of free banking:

- Permanently freeze the current monetary base.
- Allow private banks to issue their own notes.
- Mandate that banks allow depositors to opt in to 100% reserve accounts free of charge.
- Mandate that banks offering fractional-reserve accounts make public key information. These might include reserve rates, asset classes being used to back deposits, and compensation offered in the event of a suspension of payment but they could be decided by an appointed panel.
- Government sells all gold reserves and allows banks to issue notes backed by gold (or any other commodity).
- Government rescinds all taxes on the use of gold as a medium of exchange.
- Repeal legal tender laws so people can choose which currencies to accept as payment.

Over two months – the end of central banking:

- The Bank of England ceases its open-market operations and no longer finances government debt.
- The Bank of England is privatised (it may well remain as a central clearing house).

This reform swiftly establishes a free banking system and the monetary context for honest politics. Large-scale depositors will have been bailed in to banks as shareholders in what remain investment vehicles. Not stated in Evans's summary is Dowd's proposal to extend bank directors' liability which I brought forward in my Financial Institutions (Reform) Bill.

Unlike the Huerta de Soto plan, fractional-reserve demand deposits are permitted and there is therefore no provision to expropriate banks in such a manner as to offset public liabilities. In an environment without taxpayer-backed deposit insurance, however, it seems likely that 100% reserve accounts would be popular. It is not clear how they would be backed by cash: perhaps banks would obtain the necessary reserves by selling assets to government in exchange for new money with a similar affect on the public finances.

Conclusion

We have lived through an era of monetary history unprecedented in the industrial age. Chronic credit expansion has significantly funded welfare states' deficit spending while eroding the stock of physical capital. We have come to a profound crisis of political economy: social democracy underpinned by easy money is ending.

That process of conclusion will be marked by a series of bubbles as desperate interventions are applied in an attempt to defibrillate stagnant economies. At some point, it will become apparent that these interventions are futile when some combination of widespread default and massive price inflation takes place. Rapid action will then be necessary to reinstate a basis for sustainable and just prosperity based on free-market capitalism without the systematic intervention in money and bank credit which is even now bringing us to calamity.

Finally, it is food for thought that Dave Fishwick, a van and minibus entrepreneur, has substantially invented an appropriate popular model without recourse to high theory or obedience to state regulation.

MAKING COMPETITION WORK

Baroness Kramer

Between now and 2020, banking in the UK will go through the greatest period of change since the Big Bang. Only reform on a major scale can offer the taxpayer the assurance that a crisis like 2008 will not be repeated. Only major reform can return the banks to their fundamental role of re-allocating capital in support of the real economy.

I was asked to state my vision and this is it: By 2020 the big four banks will have shrunk to a size that is more manageable and more cost efficient. They will hold more capital and will have mechanisms in place to resolve failures without resorting to government funding. Shareholder logic will have separated retail and investment banking. Numerous new bank competitors, many focused on specific customer niches, will have entered the retail market. A new and growing network of local and community banks will be serving more deprived communities and start-up businesses.

New online platforms, peer-to-peer (P2P) and crowd funders, will have seized a significant share of the market. Large data companies from Google to Vodafone will be wondering if they should take over the transactional roles of the banking system which are, after all, just data transmission. Bank profits will have normalised. Retail banking will essentially be a utility business, while investment banking will no longer be propped up by an implicit taxpayer subsidy.

An appetite for bank reform

For this new world to have any chance politicians and regulators will need backbone. The big banks have a long history of deflecting change, capturing both politicians and regulators. Today, the appetite for bank reform is driven by fury at the 2008 financial crisis and a chain of scandals notably payment protection insurance (PPI) mis-selling and abuse of Libor. The post-mortem on these scandals has exposed deep flaws in the big banks from cultural malaise and weak corporate governance to unsustainable business models and managerial incompetence. The big banks became not just too big to fail but too large and too complex to manage. They took on too much risk, decisions were often governed by greed, they failed to invest in either staff or technology, and they forgot the customer. Five years after the financial crisis, the big banks are still failing to get adequate credit flows into the economy, especially to small businesses.

Reform is underway and it is fair to say its extent and pace has surprised even its strongest advocates. A year ago few expected that the ring-fencing and corporate governance reforms proposed by the Vickers Commission would be enacted. Even fewer would have expected the political and regulatory establishment to be legislating for more than Vickers; for example, the acceptance that the regulator should be able to split banks which do not split themselves. But, what happens when the economy turns? Bank boards will be tempted to again hire the charismatic, aggressive risk-takers whom they chose as their leaders in the pre-crisis years. The constraints of regulation will look old-fashioned and out-of-step with prosperous times. The political and regulatory establishment will find it hard to fight back as bankers assure them that the new world is risk-free.

If we want a banking system that serves our economy, we have only a small window in which to set reform resolutely in place.

True competition

The industry is so powerful and so global that reform requires action by a complex swathe of players domestic and international and involves structure, capital, regulation, corporate governance, remuneration, culture, and competition. I will limit my comments particularly to competition, an area which has often received less attention and looked less glamorous than many of the others.

Competition is the best disinfectant for the banking industry. True competition, in contrast to the virtual oligopoly that has existed, can allow the market to exert its force on the industry, not displacing regulation but as a powerful complement to it.

Customers able to move their accounts and with a real choice would surely have prevented the complete loss of customer focus and the scale of mis-selling. Empowered depositors, shifting their accounts, would have reduced the passive deposits so tempting as cheap funding for the high-risk banking activities of large institutions. Bank shareholders with a real choice might have had more institutions to compare with their own and might have noticed that the 'unbelievable' profitability of the banks was accruing not to them but to management.

We should 'let a thousand flowers bloom' rather than design a prescriptive template for banks of the future. The new or newly arrived banks in the UK offer great variety: Metro Bank focuses on customer service; Triodos (from Holland) emphasises sustainability; Handelsbanken (from Sweden) targets business and professional clients; Aldermore serves small businesses. This means reform needs to open up banking and use competition as far as possible as the mechanism to offer choice, to prevent abuse, and to protect the taxpayer. The challenge for the regulator is to use judgement to provide appropriate and proportionate regulation without stifling competition and innovation – no easy task.

This is where I want to commend the current bank regulators, the new Financial Conduct Authority and Prudential Regulation Authority. For more than a century the regulators contrived to make it impossible for any new bank applicant to get a banking license. Existing banks could be bought and re-designed but new banks were resisted. Under the Financial Services Authority (FSA), the old application process in essence required a new bank to raise all its capital, buy its technology, and employ a full set of staff before giving any indication of whether or not the application would succeed. Typically would-be applicants would get a quiet phone call recommending they withdraw their application rather than face the embarrassment of a public refusal. At the same time, new banks were treated as more risky than existing banks and were required to hold far more capital than their established counterparts.

Supporting new applications

In an FSA report issued this March, this was all changed. The new regulators have committed to a new regime which supports new applications and offers a reasonable path to an approval. The report recognises that the risks of new banks are actually lower than that of existing large banks both because they are not systemic and because recovery and resolution mechanisms can be built in from the start. If a new bank fails, and some will, this will not be a failure for the regulator so long as resolution can be achieved without harm to the taxpayer. The capital requirements for new banks will now be proportionate and lower than for many existing banks. Competition finally has a chance and we must be resolute in holding the regulators to this path.

However, new competitors will have no chance unless customers can actually shift their business. This means that we have to dismantle barriers that have been built over the years to discourage customers from changing banks. In September, new rules on seven-day account switching will make this easier. Mobile banking, which will finally arrive in 2014, will also make a difference. The government has committed to removing control of the payments system (the internal plumbing of the banking sector) from the big banks and allowing everyone to access the system under the oversight of a regulator rather than having to go through one of the big banks as is currently the case. These changes will make a difference but they may not be enough.

It is time to start considering new and radical solutions. Should all bank accounts be fully portable in the way phone numbers are? Do we try to do that through a central system or are there better alternatives? Can we get portability and also protect privacy and allow innovation? It really is time for a major piece of work in this area to lay out a roadmap to the future. For too long this has been left to the big banks which simply suit themselves. The work could be done by the payments body that, in the Chancellor's plans, will succeed the current Payments Council.

Capping market concentrations

When will we get the competition we want? Even with a new openness in the regulatory system the existing big banks will be able to limit the incomers through use of their market dominance – over 75% of current account provision and small business lending is done by the four biggest banks. New competitors will take time to grow organically and we need a fully functional banking system in the near-term to support recovery in our economy. So, I would argue that we should refer the industry to the new Competition and Markets Authority now, in contrast to the Office of Fair Trading's recommendation that it consider such a referral in a few years time. The USA sets a cap on market concentrations for its banks to force competition. I see no reason why we should not do the same.

We could start this process by splitting up the Royal Bank of Scotland (RBS), a bank in which taxpayers have an ownership stake of over 80% and which is currently under-performing. It could be divided into a 'good bank' and a 'bad bank' to separate the problem loans that are weighing it down, tying up its capital, and restricting new lending. Most of the objections to such a split are technical ones related to the non-taxpayer shareholders but they strike me as straw-men, not real barriers. Why not go further? Economies of scale peter out at something like a quarter of the size of RBS. The local focus that is so missing at present could be realised in a regional split, perhaps taking RBS back to its component parts. Competition would get a rapid helping hand.

Making space

A competitive market should also make space for alternative players. In particular we need local and community banks and credit unions. The UK has long lacked this entire layer of banking, one that could service our more deprived communities and also new start-up ventures, social enterprises, and charities. In Germany, the Sparkasse fills this role and in the USA such needs are met by community development banks, funds, and credit unions. This is more important than ever as Universal Credit now requires benefit recipients to have fully functional bank accounts and also as we try to develop both the Big Society and a new culture of enterprise.

For those who do not believe that such a vacuum in banking exists, I point to the success of the 'payday' lenders who have been able to charge extraordinary interest rates to people who in effect regard these lenders as their banking service. New legislation on disclosure should soon provide data that will give us a detailed picture of the lending gaps. Credit unions and community funds in this country are small, fragmented, and very limited in what they can offer. It will take a major commitment by charities, social enterprises, and local authorities as well as a determined government to build a proper network from these small beginnings. A roadmap is an urgent priority. I want to see legislation that requires big banks to partner in such networks in areas where they are neglecting lending, assisting with capital and technical knowledge. Such a requirement would recognise the utility role of banks and recompense the taxpayer for the role we still play as a last backstop for banks' core activities.

Finally, we need to develop the potential of the P2P lenders. These online platforms bring together individuals or firms who wish to lend to individuals or small entities that wish to borrow. The platforms provide credit analysis but the lender decides to whom to lend. This is a new industry which in the UK is eating away at the domination of banks in individual and small business lending. It is growing rapidly and increasingly setting the standard for efficient, well priced lending.

Conclusion

The industry has been pleading for regulation to keep out rogue players and such rules are finally expected in 2014. While government is welcoming these players and including them in programmes like funding-for-lending, they still live with the tax disadvantage that banks can net loan losses from their taxable earnings while individuals cannot. It's time to establish a level playing field.

Competition is one of the key mechanisms for a reformed banking sector. If the grip of the big banks is not broken, if virtually all banks offer identical services and products, if new technology remains delayed, if all individuals do not have access to basic banking services – in other words if we stay as we are today – then our economy and our communities will not achieve anything close to their potential.

LETTING MARKETS WORK

Syed Kamall

Since the onset of the economic crisis in 2008, policymakers have stumbled from one solution to another in a vain attempt to get the economy growing. The early days of the crisis were characterised by regulatory fire-fighting, as the taxpayer bailout of failing banks and the collapse of Lehman Brothers reverberated through the financial system.

The response of politicians has been like a fight breaking out in a bar. Legislators have preferred to hit those they have always wanted to hit (hedge funds and private equity) rather than those who started it (the banks and regulators that failed). Their actions over the past four years have done little to restore confidence and little to kick-start growth. As a consequence the global economy is stuttering, while some stock markets are now at levels not seen since the months before the crisis, propped up by ever greater quantities of money being printed in London and Washington.

Proof that legislators have not learned the lessons of the crisis is evident in their response to every new crisis. More than five years after the run on Northern Rock in the UK and more than four years after the collapse of Lehman Brothers, failing banks across the European Union are still being bailed out by taxpayers.

The challenge for policymakers should be to create a competitive and free market in financial services which provides its customers with choice and value, and which does not have to turn to the taxpayer for subsidy.

Reinventing a financial culture

Politicians, central bankers, and regulators were as culpable as management in allowing the banks to develop a culture of risk denial. It was central bankers around the world who reduced interest rates and ushered in an era of cheap money; it was politicians proclaiming the end of boom and bust and encouraging the growth of the mortgage bubble; and it was regulators and bank management teams who bought in to the idea that you could 'engineer' risk out of existence by using ever more complex financial instruments, like so-called mortgage-backed securities, which few people really understood. By putting in place compensation schemes and deposit guarantee schemes, individuals came to believe that their money was safe regardless of where it was invested or deposited.

We need to reinvent a culture where risks are recognised and shouldered by bankers who take responsibility and accept the consequences of the actions of their institutions. In a truly competitive market, banks and financial institutions that were over-exposed would have failed. The profitable bits of their businesses would have been bought up by rivals or new entrants and the rest left to disintegrate. Their destruction and dismemberment would have given way to newer, healthier businesses.

Unfortunately, some institutions were – and still are – deemed too big to fail. Bailing them out has done nothing to change the belief among bankers that they might yet end up with a handout from the taxpayer if they take on the wrong risks.

Paying for failure

Not only have politicians in the EU sought to ban or tax some financial activities, we have spent the past four or so years creating a vast and complex regulatory architecture to monitor the activities of banks and other financial services firms. MEPs and Commission officials proudly boast how they have replaced the EU's old supervisory architecture with a new European system of financial supervisors, consisting of three European Supervisory Authorities (ESAs): the European Banking Authority (EBA), the European Securities and Markets Authority (ESMA), and the European Insurance and

Occupational Pensions Authority (EIOPA); as well as a European Systemic Risk Board (ESRB).

Despite the mutual back-slapping as a result of these new structures, the fundamental problem remains. Banks are still failing and being bailed out by taxpayers. I would recommend four new measures to try to save the taxpayer from paying for failure and to introduce more stability into the banking system:

1. Governments need to state clearly that enough is enough: no more bank bail-outs ever.

Without sending a strong and clear message to banks that they will never again be bailed out, the bankers will not believe it. To underline this clear intention, two further policies are needed:

a) Supervisors will need to spell out procedures to wind down failing banks without taxpayer funding and to create a scheme to allow customers of failed retail banks to continue to pay their bills or withdraw money from ATMs until ownership is resolved.

b) Governments should legislate for a separation of wholesale banking activities from retail activities. At the very least, the savings of retail investors should never be used to subsidise the trading activities in the investment arms of banks. The ring-fence needs to be resilient and high, for example, as recommended in the Vickers Report in the UK and similarly by the Liikanen Commission at EU level.

A range of other proposals for separation of activities has been put forward across the globe, each with their pluses and minuses. Unfortunately, ideas like the Volcker Rule or those put forward in France and Germany appear overly complex and open to interpretation. Unlike the Vickers proposals that identify which activities and infrastructures are systemically vital to the functioning of the economy, these other proposals prohibit specific activities. If we go down this path, we will spend years working out what is and is not a 'good' or 'bad' banking activity. Not only will politicians and regulators get mired in endless ideological debate and argument, but the banks themselves will simply learn how to game the system by finding loopholes. Far simpler to say what is in the ring-fence than what is it not.

2. *Make directors more liable for failure.*

One of the main reasons for the unpopularity of the banks in recent years, and the populist wave of hostile and poorly thought-out regulation, is the perceived refusal to accept fault on the part of the bankers. It is even harder to vote out bad bankers than bad politicians!

It is unacceptable for individuals who presided over failure to avoid facing the consequences of their actions. Measures to improve corporate governance are, of course, welcome, but a far simpler and cleaner solution would be to force the management of financial institutions to take a personal interest in ensuring their employees only take risks that are reasonable.

Responsibility for the risks banks take should sit on the shoulders of the directors, who act for those putting up the risk capital. We could investigate the feasibility of returning to the partnership model where directors are directly liable for failure. Other options include paying directors in the form of bonds so that they pay the price for failure.

3. *Encourage more transparency in banking.*

Most savers are still under the belief that their savings are actually held by the bank with which they deposited them. In fact they are usually loaned out in order to generate both revenue for the bank and interest for customers. If bank customers know that institutions will be allowed to fail, then banks are more likely to make their operations and charging structures more transparent to earn their customers' trust.

Transparency should result in three styles of banking:

Deposit account or standard retail banking, where you are guaranteed to get your money back during an agreed time. You may pay a fee for this, but it is safer than stuffing your money under a mattress.

Loan or bond account banking, where the bank admits that your money is not on deposit, but is actually loaned to it in return for an agreed interest rate.

Money market or investment banking, where the money is invested in the stock market, managed funds, or other complex financial instruments. Your money can be professionally managed or customers who show they understand the risks can have the freedom to invest as they want. These accounts may yield higher returns but the downside is the value of your investment can go down as well as up – even to zero.

4. Reform accounting standards.

There is currently a debate over the need to reform the way accountants report on a company's financial health. Investor groups argue that the International Financial Reporting Standards (IFRS) which have been used prior to, during, and after the crash, have clearly not given a 'true and fair' account of a bank's balance sheet. The discount many banks are currently trading at in the markets against their stated asset value may reflect the fact that many investors lack trust in the balance sheets of banks.

Superficially, in a globalised world, it might appear to make sense to have globally converged accounting standards. However it defeats the object of ensuring financial stability if those standards are not prudentially sound. The reality is American and European accounting models serve fundamentally different purposes, the latter being more concerned with corporate governance concerns than the former. Convergence of these models in the IFRS has led each to be diluted by the other, with damaging implications.

Investors are concerned that the IFRS has encouraged a move away from the principle of prudence, whereby accounts must not overstate assets or understate liabilities, profits should only be booked once they are realised, and sufficient funds are put aside to cover any potential losses. This convention has been replaced by an American-inspired principle of auditor neutrality, which means accounts are always deemed 'true and fair' if they have ticked all the boxes required by the IFRS. This encourages auditors to move away from exercising professional scepticism when assessing a company's accounts and instead to simply tick boxes. Box-ticking failed to spot financial institutions recording expected income from complex financial instruments in advance. Financial institutions failed, or had to be bailed out, since they simply did not put aside enough funds to cover their exposure to credit default swaps and collateralised debt obligations. AIG Financial Products was able to build a portfolio of $2.7 trillion (£1.7 trillion) in derivatives, resulting in liabilities many times its capacity to pay out.

Accounting practices should be reformed to ensure they provide a genuinely 'true and fair' view of balance sheets, with appropriate levels of loan loss provisioning in place. This means returning to a system of accounting that pre-dates the convergence project in the early 1980s, before which auditors and accountants would only sign-off accounts if they were sure the company in question was a going concern. The liability implications are potentially far-reaching for auditors and directors, but this should in turn be a driver of better governance.

However, some of the big four accounting firms and those who were behind pushing the IFRS argue that this is not the role of accounts. They say accounting standards should not encourage the build-up of sums of capital to guard against potential losses. Instead they believe legislators and regulators should specify the capital buffers banks need to guard against losses. While legislators tried this with the Basel capital requirements, lobbying by large banks, especially in France and Germany, led to a dilution of these standards. Also, when banks are allowed to create their own models, it is clear they will attempt to game the system and claim their balance sheets are more robust than they might actually be.

A proper debate is needed on the role of accounting standards and to what extent they are true and fair; and prudence should be guiding principles.

Conclusion

All this will take time. Even if we were able to shift all the risk profile overnight, we still could not restructure the shape of the banking system in the same timescale. It will be a long time before we can replace the deposit-guarantee schemes with alternatives that do not place the ultimate burden on taxpayers.

But we have not yet made a proper start. It is time to get banks run again by directors who exercise a genuine duty of care to their shareholders, audited by accountants who are forced to give a true and fair view of a bank's financial health.

If we can achieve these objectives, then finally we may have learned the lessons of the crisis and go on to create a more competitive and transparent banking system, where both bankers and savers act more diligently.

GETTING THE GLOBAL RULES RIGHT

Vicky Ford

In theory, setting banking rules at a European level should be a step in the right direction for getting vital regulation right. Today's banking industry is global and to avoid arbitrage or banks' relocating, it is best that rules are set globally. In recent years G20 statements have been key in originating a global approach and are coupled with the detailed work of the Bank of International Settlements in Basel. Bringing those rules into detailed legislation through the EU's 27-member bloc should help build part of that global agreement. Yet, often it does not.

In practice, fundamental flaws with the way banking legislation is written and negotiated in the EU cause problems. The system is not one whereby an international global standard is directly transposed into EU law and then implemented via 27 sets of national laws. Instead, special pleading, political point-scoring, and horse-trading pull and tug at legal texts, which can make the final outcomes very different from what was originally intended.

This can lead to divergence from rules agreed at a global level, or rules which suit one country more than another. The level playing field is compromised as can be the integrity of the rules themselves.

Increasingly rules emerging from Europe are regulations: rules on which member states have little discretion when writing them into national law. This 'maximum harmonisation' approach makes it extremely difficult for countries to introduce their own tailored standards.

Why does this matter?

The debate surrounding hedge funds and private equity regulations under the EU's Alternative Investment Fund Manager Directive brought into sharp focus how easy it is for financial services to re-locate into other less regulated or less taxed parts of the world.

The Financial Transaction Tax (FTT) is another prime example of unilateral policies pursued to the detriment of Europe's global competitiveness. Some estimate that the latest FTT structure proposed by the Commission would significantly increase the price of debt issuance by as much as 14% and have a disproportionate effect on the cost of issuing government debt. This appears to run completely contrary to the strategy to help European companies diversify away from borrowing from banks. It will restrict funds available to the real economy and push up national debts. Furthermore, an FTT without international agreement has been proven through history to result in financial transactions relocating to other parts of the world. These examples demonstrate the need for a joined-up global approach.

However, sometimes EU legislation simply pretends it is following a global approach. For example, Basel III sets out global standards for capital, liquidity, and leverage ratios. This is being introduced within the EU through the Capital Requirements Directive and Regulation 4 (CRD4). But the EU text has many amendments which are not included in Basel III. Often these amendments give one member state an advantage over the others, undermining the common market. One of the material divergences identified by the Basel Committee is the way bank/insurance groups will be able to account for capital held in insurance subsidiaries as if it was equivalent to bank capital, when actually the insurance capital would not be equal in its ability to help cover losses. This bank-insurance conglomerate model is popular in France, whose representatives lobbied hard for the amendments. Amendments like this also undermine transparency, making it more difficult to compare banks and to understand their risks.

The EU approach also sometimes removes powers which should have stayed at a national level. In CRD4 crucial prudential tools are largely contained in the one-size-fits-all *regulation* rather than the more flexible *directive*. The legal instrument of a regulation addresses a complaint that countries sometimes do not implement the EU directives. However, the regulation tool also limits the ability for individual countries to introduce higher standards. A highly controversial discussion was the limits on macro-prudential powers at a national level. A key lesson from the crisis is surely that banks can fail for many different reasons: national regulators argued that they needed these tools to be able to reduce lending for example, in order to fend off asset bubbles.

This is especially important to countries like the UK which has such a large financial service sector and is more exposed to financial sector risks than others. The UK needs to protect the City institutions from regulatory arbitrage but it also needs to protect the UK taxpayer from the risks posed by the City. For example, to protect taxpayers' money and the domestic economy, the UK government has proposed ring-fencing retail and investment banks. Initial drafts of the EU regulation would have severely limited the ring-fence, and the final text does still put many constraints on it.

Sometimes introducing additional amendments to legislation on issues which are not agreed globally could have market-distorting affects. Shoe-horned into CRD4 was a politically expedient but practically blunt 1:1 cap on bankers' bonuses; this was subsequently amended with the option to double that to 2:1 with the consent of shareholders. If this results in larger upfront salaries, it will undermine the bigger-picture global regulatory drive to encourage a more longer-dated, risk-related approach to remuneration.

Over-regulation or regulation which is inconsistent or poorly thought through can restrict the ability of the financial sector to provide the investment vital for growth in the rest of the economy. A major concern of the insurance industry has been the potential unintended consequences of EU Solvency 2 legislation. Whilst some of their concerns have been addressed, there are still issues relating to criteria which would limit investments in lower tranches of investment-grade bonds. Infrastructure providers have suggested this could materially impact financing for infrastructure projects which tend to be structured in the BBB credit spectrum. To put it more simply, is the strengthening of insurance company legislation intended to prevent another Equitable Life-type event going to have an unintended consequence on, for example, investment in energy infrastructure?

The 'unintended consequences' effect is compounded by the fact that once something is agreed in EU law, it is very difficult to amend. This is partly because the legislative process is so clunky and partly because agreeing something between 27 member states creates a robust herd mentality: 'we agreed this between 27 countries, so it must be good'. Another blockage is often the European Commission which reacts strongly to proposals to remove or reduce a piece of EU law, citing the 'ever closer union' language in the EU treaty.

How does this happen?

The legislative process in Brussels is filled with opportunities for moulding and remoulding legislation. Even before the Commission publishes its draft legislation, interested parties lobby extensively and furiously. Once that draft is published, the text is opened up for amendments by both MEPs in the European Parliament and by the 27 finance ministries though the European Council.

In the Parliament, it is now not unusual to have well over 1000 amendments proposed. Some will be haggled away through various compromise meetings before being brought to a first vote in the Economic and Monetary Affairs Committee.

Once the Parliament Committee and the Council have both voted on their own draft text then a three-way 'trialogue' negotiation commences between the Parliament, the Council, and the Commission. In other Committees it is normal that if the legislation is not agreed within three such negotiations, it will go back to the drawing board for a second reading. On financial affairs dossiers, however, the negotiations sometimes appear unlimited. CRD4 had over 30 such meetings in a process which lasted nearly a year. Trialogue horse-trading means there can be significant changes. Last-minute compromise agreements do not allow for a transparent way to build effective regulation or to assess its impacts.

The legislative process is often poorly understood by those outside the Brussels bubble, who underestimate the powers held by MEPs who can amend and shape the text. There is a lack of transparency in the legislative process. MEPs, especially those from larger groups, often only work on limited pieces of the legislative jigsaw and re-regulate what has already been covered in another dossier.

Another serious problem is a lack of expert engagement or an effective mechanism to test the impact of amendments put forward by the Parliament or during the trialogue process. This is particularly the case with financial service dossiers. In theory, the Commission must produce impact assessments for its own proposals; in reality, these are rarely of any quality or in-depth analysis.

Things could be improved if the bodies setting global rules were more involved with those negotiating legislation. In particular, I have heard many individual MEPs and senior negotiators from the European Commission criticising the Basel Committee saying: 'We don't need to just copy Basel.' If the members of the Basel Committee want their rules to stick, they should have been on the ground helping drive their points home.

Why does this happen?

Sometimes changes introduced are made for good reason. For example, in the CRD4 debate, a number of amendments were made to try to ensure the pace of bank reform did not strangle funds available for finance in the wider economy. These were made in reaction to comments and analysis by organisations representing small and medium enterprises (SMEs) as well as those representing larger companies. The initial Basel proposals were also amended to give a more proportionate regime for trade finance, and to address concerns regarding repo markets.

Sometimes amendments stem from a different view on the pace of bank reform between the Council and the Parliament. The impact of the Eurozone crisis has left certain EU countries wanting to slow down the pace of bank reform, but MEPs have wanted to work towards the global standard. In the first votes in the Council, key

G20 commitments to a binding leverage ratio were dropped. This was re-instated by the Parliament. The Parliament's amendments also tightened up the key definition of capital itself whereas the Council text in this area had been cited as a material weakness, a divergence from the Basel rules.

Other amendments reflect differences in the way financial sectors operate in different countries or diversification in the EU banking sector. For example, as a UK MEP, I have fought hard for buy-to-let mortgages not to be effectively outlawed under EU mortgage legislation, arguing that removing them entirely could destabilise a key part of the UK residential rental market and that they should be regulated at a national level. I have worked with MEPs from many jurisdictions to table amendments recognising the building society and co-operative banking networks.

However, not all amendments in the name of diversification are laudable. I frequently come across amendments which, on deeper investigation, look like trying to get special treatment for poor practices but are proclaimed to be addressing 'EU specificities'. Supporting diversity can only be a good thing whereas changes to just merely try to tip a playing field for vested interests are not, and again undermine a global approach.

Sometimes meddling by MEPs for political reasons starts with good intentions but has vast unintended consequences. We can see this with the resolution fund currently being discussed as part of the Recovery and Resolution Directive. The Commission's proposal sets a levy based on a percentage of deposits but an amendment put forward in the Parliament would change this to a percentage of liabilities. The MEPs involved are trying to send a message that they support 'normal high-street' banks, but the amendment could increase the levy on industry by estimates of up to €500 billion. This would have a massive impact on funds available for investment and growth.

Five years after the financial crisis started, the Cyprus situation showed that Europe is still not immune from bank failures. The issue of who pays for a bank's losses when it fails is still as charged as ever. Using taxpayers' funds to pay for bailouts in other countries remains politically toxic. More politicians are beginning to understand that single European level solutions may not be the right answer, and indeed can increase moral hazard.

Add to this a political tug of war where European political institutions fight for extra powers, mix in a complex confusion about the roles of regulators and supervisors and how they interact across borders, overlay the whole debate with a rush towards a single supervisor within the Eurozone but which the UK cannot join, and you get a flavour of why it's such a mess.

What is the right way forward for reform?

The single market in financial services has had great benefits in the past: freeing up barriers to the movement of capital and thus aiding investment and growth. Many of the more recent legislative proposals, however, seem to start from a protectionist approach, and not from a free market vision.

As a UK MEP involved in the debate, I see three ways to try and improve practices. Fundamentally, it is vital to reconsider the way banking and financial services legislation is created if the UK is to stay in the single market.

First, we can try to reform the system from within, trying to better engage with the current approach. This is the current UK Treasury strategy, and it is working to an extent. The UK won key concessions on CRD4, strengthening capital rules and keeping liquidity and leverage ratios. However, this engagement could be improved; for example, if the formidable Westminster financial affairs scrutiny processes became motivated to identify issues and impacts in EU draft legislation whilst there is still time to try to make recommendations and amend the text. The UK also needs a stronger voice on business-related issues in the college of commissioners.

Secondly, and in addition, we should try and reform current processes. For example increasing the use of EU impact assessments and introducing a rapid appeal if there are unintended consequences of any piece of legislation. There should be a review of which decisions taken at EU level could be better sent back to national legislation and where to tighten up holes in EU implementation of global rules. Furthermore, there needs to be greater respect for the differences between those inside the Banking Union and those outside. For example, if the Eurozone decides to establish cross-border bailout funds there should be carve outs for non-Eurozone countries and any increases in the role of the European Banking Authority should not be forced upon those outside Banking Union.

A third step would be to negotiate special protection for the UK given its exposure to financial services. For example, the recent *Fresh Start Project* review of the UK's relationship with the EU recommends that the UK should try to negotiate a special veto on financial services legislation and describes a 'hand brake' for financial laws. Those arguing against this have said the UK would never be outvoted 26 to 1 in the European Council on a financial services dossier. However, the vote on bonuses structures was exactly that. If issues like sharing bailout funds went to a vote, this would be an even bigger and more divisive issue.

Finally, we need to make it clear that unless there is reform, leaving the EU is a likely outcome. The Prime Minister has warned that the future of the UK in Europe is already a very narrow decision. Even with the drawback of the EU legislative process for the financial sector, leaving the EU is not a clear-cut solution. The UK would still be affected by laws made in the EU. Furthermore, in the banking sector especially, many affected businesses argue forcefully that they wish the UK to stay as a strong voice inside the single market.

However, the future direction of banking legislation and regulation is a key part of the monetary/fiscal/banking union which the UK has stated it will not be part of. To stay in the single market, the UK will need very clear lines drawn between it and the Eurozone countries. Decisions taken to try to protect the Eurozone cannot be cut and pasted on to all 27 countries.

Being ready to take the terminal step and walk away from the Union may sound drastic. To some, the technicalities of the legislative process in Brussels may sound like an arcane topic not worthy of such explosive action. But as the cliché goes: the devil is in the detail. If these details are not right, we must take action to try to guarantee the integrity of the vital rules set at a global level, to protect ourselves from risks at a domestic level, and to prevent the economic consequences of poorly thought out actions. If we do not, in future we could look back on the crises we are seeing now and regret missed opportunities.

CONTRIBUTOR BIOGRAPHIES

Steve Baker has been Conservative MP for Wycombe since 2010. He established and chairs the All-party Parliamentary Group on Economics, Money, and Banking. He also co-founded the Cobden Centre, a think-tank concerned with money and social progress. Before becoming an MP, Steve was an engineer officer with the Royal Air Force.

Sharon Bowles was elected Liberal Democrat MEP for the South-East of England in 2005. Since 2009, she has chaired the European Parliament's Economic and Monetary Affairs Committee. She was also shadow rapporteur on the Capital Requirements Directive and Regulation 4. Before turning to politics, Sharon was a patent attorney.

Vicky Ford has been Conservative MEP for the East of England since 2009. She is a member of the European Parliament's Economic and Monetary Affairs Committee and was also shadow rapporteur for the Capital Requirements Directive and Regulation 4. Vicky spent 14 years working in banking, most at JP Morgan, before becoming managing director of Bear Sterns International's loan capital markets division between 2001 and 2003.

Mark Garnier has been Conservative MP for Wyre Forest since 2010. He sits on the Treasury Select Committee and is a member of the Parliamentary Commission on Banking Standards. Before becoming an MP, he spent 18 years working in banking and finance. In 1999, Mark set up his own investment management business, Severn Capital, of which he remains a partner and a shareholder.

Tony Greenham is an economist, chartered accountant and former investment banker who leads research into financial sector reform at **nef** (the new economics foundation). He is a regular media commentator and public speaker on money and banking, and is co-author of many articles, reports and books on the subject including *Where Does Money Come From? A guide to the UK monetary and banking system.*

Damian Horton is an investment professional, with a background in investment banking and asset management across a number of financial products, including structuring, trading, and managing collateralised debt obligations. He is also a Chartered Financial Accountant. More recently, he has been researching and developing new concepts for investing, touching on crowd-funding, co-operatives, and private equity.

David Jackman is the founder of The Ethics Foundation, a director of The Ethical Space and chair of the British Standards Institute's Sustainable Communities Committee. Part of the management team which established the Financial Services Authority, he was head of education and ethics when he left the regulator in 2003. David was the first chief executive of the Financial Services Skills Council (now the Financial Skills Partnership) and is a non-executive director at Hornbuckle Mitchell.

Dr Syed Kamall was elected Conservative MEP for London in 2005. He is a member of the European Parliament's Economic and Monetary Affairs Committee and was shadow rapporteur on the Alternative Investment Fund Managers Directive. Before election as an MEP, he worked as a marketing, strategy, and public affairs consultant. Syed is also co-founder of the Global Business Research Institute.

Baroness Kramer was elevated to 'the other place' in December 2010, before which she was Liberal Democrat MP for Richmond Park. She is co-chair of the party's Treasury Parliamentary Policy Committee and a member of the Parliamentary Commission on Banking Standards. She established Infrastructure Capital Partners in the 1990s and remains a director and shareholder.

Andrea Leadsom has been Conservative MP for South Northamptonshire since 2010. She is a member of the Treasury Select Committee and spent ten years at BZW and Barclays working in swaps, project finance, and structured products, rising to financial institutions director. Andrea has also worked at a hedge fund and spent ten years as head of corporate governance and senior investment officer at Invesco Perpetual.

Chris Leslie was elected Labour MP for Nottingham East in 2010, having represented Shipley as an MP from 1997 to 2005. Between his two stints in the House, he was a director at the New Local Government Association. Before becoming an MP, he worked as a political researcher. Chris is now Shadow Financial Secretary to the Treasury.

Andy Love has been Labour MP for Edmonton since 1997. He is a member of the Treasury Select Committee and the Parliamentary Commission on Banking Standards. He managed a small import-export firm in the mid-1970s before becoming secretary of the London Co-operative Political Committee. He was then elected as a Haringey councillor.

John Mann was elected Labour MP for Bassetlaw in 2001. He has been a member of the Treasury Select Committee since 2009, having previously been a member between 2003 and 2005. He has a background in education and research within trade unions. After branding the Parliamentary Commission on Banking Standards a 'whitewash', John launched his own inquiry into the banking industry.

John Thurso has been Liberal Democrat MP for Caithness, Sutherland, and Easter Ross since 2001. He is a member of the Parliamentary Commission on Banking Standards and the Treasury Select Committee. He was the Shadow Business Secretary until 2010. John has extensive experience in the hospitality industry including six years as chief executive of the Champneys Group.

Editor's biography

Steve Tolley has worked as a journalist for *BBC News*, *The Politics Show*, and *Money Marketing*, a financial trade paper. In his time at *Money Marketing*, Steve covered the establishment of the UK's new regulators, the work of the Independent Commission on Banking, and the regulatory structures and rules being devised in Europe. In 2011, he won Santander's *Personal Finance Trade Newcomer of the Year* award. Steve has also advised Labour's Shadow Treasury Minister Chris Leslie on bank policy.

NOTES

Notes

Notes

Notes